HANNIBAL

ANCIENTS IN ACTION

Catullus
Amanda Hurley

Cleopatra
Susan Walker and Sally-Ann Ashton

Hannibal
Robert Garland

Horace
Philip D. Hills

Lucretius
John Godwin

Martial
Peter Howell

Ovid: Love Songs
Genevieve Liveley

Ovid: Myth and Metamorphosis
Sarah Annes Brown

Pindar
Anne Pippin Burnett

Sappho
Marguerite Johnson

Spartacus
Theresa Urbainczyk

Tacitus
Rhiannon Ash

ANCIENTS IN ACTION

HANNIBAL

Robert Garland

BRISTOL CLASSICAL PRESS

This impression 2011
First published in 2010 by
Bristol Classical Press
An imprint of Bloomsbury Academic
Bloomsbury Publishing Plc
50 Bedford Square, London WC1B 3DP

A catalogue record for this book is available
from the British Library.

ISBN 978 1 8539 9725 9

Typeset by Ray Davies
Printed and bound in Great Britain by
CPI Group (UK) Ltd, Croydon, Surrey

www.bloomsburyacademic.com

Contents

For Catherine, who interrupted my
pointless journey across the Alps

List of Illustrations

Maps and plans

Figures

Was there ever a cause too lost,
Ever a cause that was lost too long
Or that showed for the lapse of time too vain
For the generous tears of youth and song?
Robert Frost, 'Hannibal', 1928

Introduction

It was not because of any driving passion but at the generous prompting of Deborah Blake at Duckworth that I undertook to write this short biography of Hannibal. I certainly had not lived with the thought of him previously. Once I had begun, however, his life engrossed me, compounded as it is equally of unrivalled success and colossal failure. Few have achieved more with such devastating consequences for the cause they supported. But he also tested the limit of what a man can do. In the end, I am in awe of him, not least because he stayed the course, and I hope I've been able to convey at least some of the admiration I have for him in this short book.

Military historians from antiquity onwards have been fascinated by topographical questions such as where Hannibal crossed the Rhône and which pass he took over the Alps. And not just military historians, of course. Leonard Cottrell in the introduction to *Hannibal: Enemy of Rome* (New York 1960) reports that while retracing Hannibal's path through France he came across a café named 'Le Relais d'Annibal' beside the River Drôme. When he asked the *patronne* why it was so called, she replied, '*Voilà la route, monsieur, la route d'Annibal.*' I confess I have nothing to add to such debates. Instead I've attempted as much as possible to examine and evaluate Hannibal's success and failure from his own perspective, in the belief that it is the business of a historian not only to present facts but also to imagine possibilities; that is, to engage with reflections about events, as well as with the events themselves. But though I've written this book from the perspective of Hannibal, and with enormous respect for his will power and dogged determination, let me also state that I am no less in admiration of his Roman adversaries for their unflinching determination to see him off the field.

I've included references to my ancient sources throughout, hoping they'll assist further investigation. Very special thanks go to Warren Wheeler, for help with photography; to Michael Holobosky for his care and patience with the maps and plans; to Annette Goldmacher for expert help with proofreading; and to Paul Cartledge, *il miglior fabbro*, for reading the manuscript at any early stage and making many suggestions and corrections. I'd also like to thank friends at Colgate and elsewhere for the stimulus of their conversation and ideas, notably Tony Aveni, Peter Balakian, Richard Garland, Drew Keller, John Gallucci, Kiko Galvez, John Naughton, Alan Swensen and Robert Wilson. As ever, I'm enormously grateful to my colleagues in the Classics Department, Rebecca Ammerman, Naomi Rood and Bill Stull, for helping to construct a shared vision of the importance of the ancient world. The faults and inaccuracies are mine alone.

Chronology

247   Birth of Hannibal; his father Hamilcar is sent as general to Sicily.

241   End of the First Punic War; Carthage is forced to give up Sicily.

238   Rome annexes Sardinia; Hamilcar is given command of Carthaginian forces in Spain.

237   Hannibal accompanies his father to Spain; according to tradition Hamilcar makes his son take an oath of eternal enmity to Rome.

229/8 Death of Hamilcar; Hasdrubal ('The Fair') is given command of Carthaginian forces in Spain.

228   Hasdrubal founds Carthago Nova (Cartagena).

227?   Rome makes an agreement with Saguntum.

226   Rome concludes the Ebro Treaty with Hasdrubal, limiting Carthaginian influence in Spain to the region south of the river.

221   Following the assassination of Hasdrubal, Hannibal is given command of Carthaginian forces in Spain; he attacks the Olcades and spends the winter in Carthago Nova.

219   Hannibal makes a surprise attack upon Saguntum; Roman envoys travel to Spain to negotiate with him but he refuses to meet them; Saguntum falls after an eight-month siege.

218   Carthage rejects a Roman ultimatum, thereby instigating the outbreak of the Second Punic War; Hannibal departs for Italy from Carthago Nova some time between late April and mid-June; he crosses the Pyrenees in July or August, the Rhône a month or so later; and the Alps in late autumn; he descends into Italy some time between mid-October and late November; defeats the Romans under P. Cornelius Scipio at the River Ticinus in late November or early December and at the River Trebbia in late December or early January.

13

217	Hannibal winters in Cisalpine Gaul; loses the sight of one eye from an infection contracted in the marshes of the River Arno; defeats the consul C. Flaminius at Lake Trasimene on 21 June; the Roman Senate appoints Q. Fabius Maximus as dictator.
216	Hannibal defeats both consular armies at Cannae on 2 August; Capua, where he winters, secedes to the Carthaginians; Hannibal's brother Mago occupies southern Italy, where there are large-scale defections to the Carthaginians.
215	Hasdrubal is prevented from joining his brother by suffering a defeat at Ibera in Spain; Hannibal concludes a treaty with Philip V of Macedon; he fails to take either Nola or Cumae; the Carthaginian general Bomilcar lands at Locri Epizephyrii with reinforcements; Hannibal winters in Apulia.
214	The Romans begin besieging Syracuse; Hannibal fails to take Tarentum.
213	The Romans recover Arpi in Apulia.
212	Hannibal captures the lower town of Tarentum, Metapontum, Thurii and Heraclea; the Romans besiege Capua; M. Claudius Marcellus captures Syracuse from the Carthaginians despite Archimedes' ingeniousness.
211	Hannibal marches on Rome but does not lay siege to it; the Romans recover Capua; Gnaeus and Publius Scipio are defeated and killed in Spain; the Carthaginians recover a part of Spain.
210	The younger P. Cornelius Scipio is made commander in Spain; now or the following year he captures Carthago Nova; the Carthaginians are driven out of Samnium and Sicily.
209	Twelve Latin colonies refuse to supply contingents for Rome; Q. Fabius Maximus recaptures Tarentum.
208	Hannibal ambushes and kills both consuls near Venusia in Lucania.
207	Hasdrubal, having finally arrived in Italy with reinforcements for his brother, is defeated and killed at the River Metaurus on 22 June.
206	The Romans recover Lucania; Scipio defeats the Carthaginians at Ilipa (near Seville), thereby ending Carthaginian rule in Spain.

205   Hannibal's brother Mago lands at Genoa in Liguria with reinforcements; Hannibal inscribes an account of his deeds in the temple of Juno Lacinia at Croton in Bruttium; the Romans make peace with Philip V of Macedon.

204   Scipio lands in Africa and unsuccessfully besieges Utica.

203   Scipio defeats Hasdrubal son of Gisgo and the Numidian king Syphax at the battle of the Great Plains in the spring; the Carthaginian Senate recalls Hannibal to Africa; the Romans defeat Hannibal's brother Mago, who dies of a wound; the Carthaginians sue for peace and a temporary truce is called.

202   The Carthaginians violate the truce; Scipio defeats Hannibal at Zama probably on 19 October.

201   Carthage surrenders; Rome imposes very harsh peace terms.

196   Hannibal is elected suffete; he introduces reforms to curb corruption.

195   Roman envoys arrive in Carthage; Hannibal flees to the eastern Mediterranean; at Ephesus he offers his services to the Seleucid king Antiochus III.

192   Hannibal accompanies Antiochus III in his campaign against the Romans in mainland Greece.

191   The Romans defeat Antiochus III at Thermopylae in the spring.

190   The Rhodians get the better of Hannibal in a naval engagement off Side in southern Turkey.

190 or 189   The Romans defeat Antiochus at Magnesia in Turkey; Hannibal flees.

189-187   Hannibal visits both Armenia, where he allegedly helps king Artaxias found a city called Artaxata, and Crete (though not necessarily in this order).

187   Hannibal seeks refuge with Prusias I of Bithynia; he commands his fleet against Eumenes II of Pergamum in the Sea of Marmara.

183 or 182   T. Quinctius Flamininus persuades Prusias I to hand over his famous guest to the Romans, but Hannibal pre-empts his arrest by taking poison.

149-146   Third Punic War; destruction of Carthage.

1

The Man

I might as well admit it from the start: we know so little about the man. There is virtually nothing in the record that sheds any light on his personality, other than what goes under the general heading of what he 'must have been'; that is, naturally endowed with all those sterling qualities that made him such a fearless and compelling leader and one of the most brilliant military tacticians of all time. The trouble with these assumptions, however plausible, is that what must have been is not the same as what was. Since Hannibal was almost constantly on the move, it is very difficult even to *conceive* of his life, other than to acknowledge that it was characterised by unrelieved harshness, deprivation and discomfort to a degree that most of us are incapable of imagining. The Roman historian Cassius Dio is surely right to state that 'hardship hardened him and lack of sleep strengthened him' (fragment 54). He lived in perpetual fear of his life – including, I suspect, during the five years when he was living in Carthage after the end of the Second Punic War before he went into permanent exile. He has left us no memoirs and his inner world is a complete blank.

It is easily overlooked that when he blindsided (forgive the pun) the Romans, defeating them three times within the space of eighteen months, he was himself already half-blind, having lost at least the partial sight of one eye as the result of an infection. Even if he had done nothing more with his life than bring his army and, most memorably, his elephants, across the highest mountain range in

Europe and down into Italy, that achievement alone would have guaranteed him a unique place in history. In the Punic (or Carthaginian) tongue his name was Hnb'l, which means 'Ba'al is my grace' or 'Ba'al has given me grace' or 'He who finds favour with Ba'al', Ba'al being the foremost Punic deity. Hnb'l was indeed touched by a god.

He was born in 247, five or six years before the end of the First Punic War, which resulted in Carthage's defeat at the hands of the Romans and the consequent loss of Sicily. He was named after his grandfather, a practice that was widespread among ancient societies and one that continues to this day in the region. His father, Hamilcar Barca, was a Carthaginian aristocrat. It was he who was largely responsible for bringing southern Spain (roughly modern Andalusia) under Carthaginian control. Nothing is known about his mother, though it is quite possible that Hannibal was of mixed race, it being common practice for Carthaginians to marry foreigners. The Barcids – 'Barca' means 'thunderbolt' – were one of the most prestigious and venerable Punic families and Hannibal seems to have inherited a very considerable fortune from his father, not that he had much leisure to enjoy it. He probably owned estates at Leptis Minor, otherwise known as Leptis Minus (modern Lamta or Lemta), in the Tripolitanian region of Libya, where he rested up for several months in 203 before the final showdown with his formidable Roman adversary, Publius Cornelius Scipio, at the Battle of Zama.

Virtually nothing is known about his early years. His father had assumed command of the Carthaginian war effort in the northwest corner of Spain shortly after his birth, so he was probably left behind in the care of his mother. At the age of nine, however, his father decided to take him to Spain. It may be that his mother had died and that there was no other trusted family member to leave him with. Even if his mother was still alive when he left, it is unlikely that he ever saw her again. So his father's influence and example were paramount.

18

1. The Man

Apart from the famous story of his swearing an oath of undying hatred to Rome (see below), no anecdotes have come down to us about his childhood such as enliven the biographies of the famous Greeks and Romans that the Greek biographer and philosopher Plutarch compiled under the title of *Parallel Lives*. We do not know what kind of education he received, though given the fact that from nine onwards he lived a military life, it must have been (*sic*) somewhat rudimentary, at least in the conventional sense of the word 'education'. Even so, he probably grew up somewhat 'hellenised', as he became highly proficient in the Greek language. His first-century BC Roman biographer Nepos (*Hannibal* 13) tells us that a Spartan called Sosylus, who accompanied him on his campaign to Italy, taught him *litterae Graecae,* which means both 'the Greek language' and 'Greek literature'. Nepos also claims that, besides being a regular correspondent, Hannibal wrote 'several books in Greek'. One was an address to the people of Rhodes, demonstrating the ruthlessness of the Romans. We also have a papyrus fragment, tentatively dated to 190-185 BC, fallaciously purporting to be a letter that 'the king of the Carthaginians', as Hannibal is styled, wrote to the Athenians. Hannibal probably knew some Latin, though he certainly was not fluent in the tongue. Livy says that the Carthaginians had difficulty in pronouncing Latin names, and since he records an instance when a misunderstanding occurred between Hannibal and one of his Italian guides, it is evident that he was no exception to the rule (22.13.6).

He must have been (*sic* again!) a man of colossal will-power – unexcelled, if not unrivalled, in the annals of antiquity. Ancient historians mainly give him his due. The Greek historian Polybius, who greatly admired his military qualities, reserves most of his criticism for Hannibal's conduct at the beginning of his career. He was particularly outraged at Hannibal's rejection of the Roman demand not to lay siege to the town of Saguntum. 'Hannibal was totally unreasonable and given to outbursts of violent anger,' he writes.

'That's why he resorted to specious arguments that had no basis in fact' (3.15.9). This assessment should be treated with caution. For one thing we do not know whether Hannibal decided on his own initiative to besiege Saguntum. Polybius talks of *sunedroi* being in his train at this point (cf. 3.20.8, 71.5). Very likely these were representatives of the Carthaginian Senate, whom he consulted before taking major decisions.

The Roman historian Livy also provides a brief character sketch, projected partly through the eyes of Hannibal's veterans (21.4). After reporting that Hannibal won the support of the entire Carthaginian army as soon as he arrived in Spain and stating that he was the spitting image of his father, he alleges that he combined reckless daring (*audacia*) with judgement (*consilium*). He goes on to state that Hannibal was energetic, able to withstand extremes of temperature, and moderate in his consumption of food and drink. He took his sleep when he could and underwent the same privations as his men. All this looks suspiciously like the stock characterisation of the ideal general, which in turn derives from the stock characterisation of the ideal philosopher. Then, speaking in his own voice, Livy charges Hannibal with a formidable list of crimes, including 'inhuman cruelty, perfidy worse than that of an ordinary Carthaginian, disregard for truth and sanctity, lack of fear for the gods, contempt for the sanctity of an oath, and absence of any religious scruples'. 'Perfidy worse than that of an ordinary Carthaginian' speaks volumes. Not for the last time in this story racism rears its head. The charge was probably based partly on the fact that he used unconventional tactics against the Romans. However, Livy was by no means lacking in admiration for the man. Alluding to the death of his brother Hasdrubal, he writes, 'I'm inclined to believe that Hannibal was more wonderful when facing adversity than he was when enjoying success' (28.12.3). It is an extraordinarily moving tribute to Rome's most deadly enemy, particularly as it comes from the quill of Rome's most patriotic historian. But how much of Livy's portrait is trustworthy? The qualities that he ascribes to Hannibal might apply to any successful military leader, whereas the vices may well have been prompted by Livy's half-unconscious desire to portray him as something of a villain. 'Punic perfidy' is a particularly objectionable charge. And when Livy accuses Hannibal of not respecting the gods, we have to wonder whose gods he is referring to.

Silius Italicus, writing two generations later than Livy, also provided a character sketch of sorts in his epic poem about the Second Punic War. It adds nothing new and reads very much like a re-working of Livy (*Punica* 1.56-60):

> Hannibal was both energetic and untrustworthy. He was the world's most accomplished deceiver and he abused the notion of justice. Once armed for battle, he showed no respect for the gods. His virtue was of a perverted sort and he despised the honourable condition of peace. A thirst for human blood inflamed him at the core of his being.

The charge of bloodthirstiness had been previously levelled against him by Seneca the Younger: seeing a trench full of human blood, Hannibal is said to have exclaimed breezily, 'What a gorgeous spectacle!' (*On Anger* 2.5.4). Whether this is true or not, he is unlikely to have been shy of inflicting extreme punishment. The hapless guide who inadvertently sent him to Casilinum instead of Casinum was first scourged and then crucified 'to instill terror in the rest' or as we might phrase it, *pour encourager les autres* (Livy 22.13.7-9). It was an intemperate reaction, to be sure, but Casilinum lay 40 miles southwest of Casinum, so the error was hardly trivial. 'Where the heck are we?' Hannibal demanded of the guide, as he looked up at the mountains and down at the rivers enclosing the plain in which he found himself.

Whether Hannibal was bloodthirsty by the standards of the day is more to the point. When he took Salmantica in 220 and Saguntum in 219, he stipulated that the free inhabitants could depart with their clothing, on condition that they left behind their weapons, their personal possessions and their slaves (Plutarch, *Moral Precepts* 248F; Livy 21.13.7). This was contrary to normal practice following a successful siege, whereby the victor would execute all the men and enslave the women and children.

Charging him with cruelty obviously served the purposes of Roman propaganda, particularly since Hannibal tried to score points with Rome's allies in the early years of the war by demonstrating leniency to his non-Roman prisoners. Later, however, as the exigencies of a protracted campaign bore down upon him, he may well have become more ruthless. Even so, Polybius reports that the acts of brutality that were perpetrated in Italy by the Carthaginians were essentially the work of one of his subordinates, namely Hannibal Monomachus or 'Fighter of single battles' (9.24.5-8). Though he does not indicate whether Hannibal made any attempt to restrain the excesses of Monomachus (no relative to our man), he does tell us that he rejected the suggestion that he should accustom his soldiers to eat human flesh as a way of surviving the journey to Italy. Polybius also accuses him of cupidity, though he does not provide any anecdote in support of his charge: he merely claims that love of money was a Carthaginian 'characteristic' (9.25.4). In Petronius' *Satyricon* Trimalchio describes him as 'a great knave and trickster', who, having captured Troy (!), melted down all the gold, silver and bronze sculptures that he could lay his hands on in order to fill his coffers (50.5). By the first century AD, it seems, Hannibal's name had become a byword for all manner of duplicity and greed.

Interestingly, none of our surviving sources charge him with lasciviousness. Pompeius Trogus (epitomised in Justin 32.4.11) says that in the treatment of his female captives he was 'so continent as to make one doubt that he had been born in Africa' – another instance of racist bias. Yet the fact that the remark is racist makes it all the more credible.

We hear next to nothing about his relations with either men or women, other than the report that before leaving Spain he married an Iberian girl from the town of Castulo in modern Andalusia. That is virtually all we know about her. The epic poet Silius Italicus (*Punica* 3.66-7) claims that the union produced a baby boy, who was born during the siege of Saguntum in 219, but he may have fabricated him to include a scene in which Hannibal transmits his hatred of Rome to his son in accordance with family tradition. We hear nothing about either his wife or his son after his return to Carthage in 203. We do not know if he had any close friends or confidants. How close, we may justly wonder, was he to his two brothers?

Hannibal was an inspirational leader: that much at least is beyond dispute. Throughout his campaign in Italy – some fifteen years in all – we never hear of any mutinies in his army. Though thousands had abandoned his cause by the time he reached the Alps, only twice, so far as we know, did small units desert once he had descended into Italy. This is all the more remarkable in light of the fact that his army consisted of a medley of races – Africans, Spanish, Ligurians, Celts, Phoenicians, Italians and Greeks – 'a mixture scraped together from all the nations of the earth', in Livy's (28.12.3-4) memorable phrase, 'differing from one another in the laws they follow, in their customs, their languages, their appearance and dress, their arms, their religious rites and observances, and – one might almost say – in the gods they worshipped'. He continues: 'Yet somehow he united them in a common bond so that there was no fighting among them nor any mutiny staged against their general, even though pay and provisions were often lacking when they were in Italy.' His men surely adored him to stick with him to the bitter end, long after the failure of the Italian campaign had become evident to all.

He was a lateral thinker with a natural aptitude to think outside the box, as his application of unconventional military tactics reveals time and again. He was also a keen student of human nature, who consistently sought to familiarise himself with the personalities of his opponents and who then exploited their weaknesses to bring about their ruin. It is obvious that he had neither the time nor the energy nor the space nor the resources nor, I suspect, the appetite for the ceremonial PR so beloved of the Romans. His distinguished adversary, the younger Publius Cornelius Scipio, the only Roman who ever defeated him in battle, was both his most accomplished and his most assiduous pupil.

Unsurprisingly, he is credited with what Livy (35.14.12) calls, not unflatteringly, 'Punic cleverness' – a mixture of sophistication and humour. Observing that his men had become demoralised by the daunting challenge of crossing the Alps, he observed that the envoys who had arrived in their camp from a Gallic tribe with an offer of assistance 'had not got across the Alps by using wings' (21.29-30). More memorably, when an officer of his called Gisgo expressed amazement at the size of the Roman army at Cannae, he commented, 'Something more amazing has escaped your notice – among all that number not one is called Gisgo' (Plutarch, *Fabius* 15.2). Though these remarks hardly make one split one's sides with laughter, they do reveal a ready wit that may have served him well in a tight spot, by taking the tension out of the air.

We have no idea what he looked like. Some scholars think that the image on the silver coinage that he issued to pay his troops before departing for Italy shows a self-portrait. It depicts a beardless man facing left on the obverse and a horse with a palm tree behind on the reverse (Fig. 1). It would certainly have been politically astute to promulgate his image through coinage. Furthermore, the Hellenistic monarchs who preceded him chronologically had provided many such precedents. But even if the image is a self-portrait, it may well be idealised. Unlike Alexander the Great, Hannibal, so far as we

Fig. 1. Silver shekel from the mint of Carthago Nova. Obverse: possible head of Hannibal; reverse: horse and palm tree.

know, never commissioned an 'official' life-size portrait of himself in stone or bronze. As the Romans never defeated him on Italian soil, they did not have much chance to appropriate any Carthaginian booty until they defeated and killed his brother Hasdrubal in 207. So it is safe to conclude that the overwhelming majority of them would have been quite unable to visualise the face of the man they so greatly feared, even if some coins with a likeness did pass into their hands.

The best one can say about a marble head in the Archaeological Museum in Naples that was reportedly found at Capua in 1667 (Fig. 2) is that it *may* have been intended to represent Hannibal. The identification is based partly on its alleged find-spot (Capua sided with Hannibal during the Second Punic War) and partly on the style of the helmet. There are, however, suspicions that it was carved in the Renaissance. And even if it is ancient and even if it is intended to represent Hannibal, the odds are that the portrait is entirely imaginary, since the style suggests that it was executed at least a century after his death. That said, the pensive and withdrawn expression in the eyes gives it a convincingly realistic appearance, and as the study of a man who failed to achieve his life's ambition it could hardly be

25

Fig. 2. Roman bust of Hannibal. Date uncertain.

bettered. In the absence of any preferable alternative, it is this head, set on a modern bust and clothed in a Roman-style military cloak or *paludamentum*, that biographers of Hannibal most commonly choose for the cover of their books.

We know nothing about his stature or build, though he surely had the constitution of an ox to survive the punishing ordeal of unrelieved camp conditions on foreign soil year after year. He sustained a serious wound to the thigh in Spain early in 219, and was wounded again two years later (Livy 21.7.10; 57.8). We hear of no other injuries but

26

it would be remarkable indeed, given his utter fearlessness, if he was otherwise unscathed. To our best knowledge his health and mental faculties remained unimpaired to the end of his life, though it is not impossible, given the tragic downward spiral of his life, that he descended into some kind of private horror towards the end. How, one might wonder, did he manage to stay sane?

Hannibal had three older sisters. Their names, as is common in antiquity, are unrecorded. He also had two younger brothers, Hasdrubal and Mago, born around 244 and 240 respectively. One other family member deserves attention: Hanno, son of Bomilcar, Hannibal's nephew, who accompanied him to Italy. The influence of Hamilcar the father on all three sons was profound. Valerius Maximus (9.3.ext. 2) reports him as saying: 'I am rearing these lion cubs for the destruction of Rome.' Likewise Nepos affirms that hatred of Rome was the father's chief 'legacy' to his son (*Hannibal* 1.3). It took the form of the famous oath that Hamilcar made his son swear on the altar of Ba'al before he agreed to allow him to accompany him to Spain. The critical words were 'that he, Hannibal, would never be a friend of the Romans'. Hatred, we are to believe, was in his bloodline and it seemingly remained undiminished even after his defeat at Zama. Both Polybius (3.11) and Nepos (*Hannibal* 1.2-6) claim that Hannibal told the anecdote about the oath-taking to the Seleucid king Antiochus III after his flight from Carthage in 195 to prove that he was psychologically programmed to take up the cudgels yet one more time. It eventually did the trick and the king engaged his services. Nepos plausibly states that hatred towards Rome meant so much to him that he was prepared to sacrifice his soul (*anima*) sooner than renounce it. We should not assume that the soul of a pagan is any less precious to its owner than is a Christian soul.

Hannibal spent most of his life abroad. He may have returned to Africa for a short spell (or spells) while accompanying his father in Spain, but we do not know this for a fact. If he did not return, he was absent for 35 years – well over half his life. He surely experienced a severe culture shock when he set foot back in Carthage. During his long years away he had been sustained in part, I suspect, by an idealised image of the city. His homecoming probably dispelled many cherished illusions. Though he may have maintained some important political allegiances during his years abroad, he can hardly have had any close allies. In a very profound sense he was a stranger in a strange land, as alien to Carthaginian society as Carthaginian society was to him.

Foremost among his enemies was Hanno (known as 'the Great', seemingly a family name), the leader of the anti-Barcid faction, who tried to oppose his appointment as commander in Spain in 221. Livy would have us believe that Hanno was still alive in 203, but this is doubtful (30.20.4). Hanno repeatedly blocked efforts to provide Hannibal with reinforcements. He therefore should, if Hannibal himself is to be believed, be held in part responsible for the failure of the Italian campaign. Though Hanno's opposition was motivated primarily by a pragmatic difference in policy, interfamilial rivalries also played their part. He had claimed that Hannibal's father was a pederast (Livy 21.3.4).

Surely the best years of Hannibal's life were between 218 and 216, when he seemed poised to stifle Rome. He was then in his late twenties. He would live for about another 35 years. What I call in this book 'the wilderness years', the period from 216 to 203, would have tested his physical and psychological reserves to the maximum. By the time he left Italy he had lost both brothers. It may well be there was no one in the world left to trust.

It is greatly to Hannibal's credit that he was able to face down his detractors after his defeat at Zama, and he deserves high marks for tackling the economic and social problems that Carthage faced at the end of the war. He might well have turned its military fortunes around even at this point, had his enemies not colluded with the

Romans. Banished, he simply picked up at the place at which he had left off before Zama – by renewing his deathless struggle against the Romans. It was the only purpose to life he perhaps understood. He finally committed suicide at the ripe old age (for those days) of 62 or 63. Such an end was certainly preferable to falling into the hands of the Romans and being humiliatingly paraded in triumph through the streets of Rome before being garrotted in the squalor of Rome's fetid underground prison, which was the fate of Julius Caesar's great adversary, the Gallic chieftain Vercingetorix. The same year allegedly saw the death of Scipio, now styled 'Africanus' in honour of his African campaign (Polybius 23.12-14; Livy 39.50.10-11; Fig. 11, p. 112). Though the coincidence in the date is entirely possible, ancient chronographers delighted in fabricating synchronisms and we should take this one with a grain of salt.

To use an overworked phrase, Hannibal was a force of nature, a man not afraid to take on its elements, embattled throughout life in both senses of the term. He was also one of history's greatest failures, epitomising the sometimes terrifying disparity between human effort and achievement. He therefore stands as a stark warning for anyone who dreams big and is in love with the impossible.

It would have been an inestimable privilege to have known him.

2

The Witnesses

There are no surviving accounts by any witnesses as such. Most critically, we do not have any word from the Carthaginian side about Hannibal. This is hugely to our disadvantage because it means that it is virtually impossible to arrive at a balanced assessment of his character and campaign. Nor do we have any writings from Hannibal himself. He did, however, erect a bronze pillar with an inscription in both Greek and Phoenician on an altar that he dedicated near the temple of Juno Lacinia (or Licinia) on Cape Colonna in the extreme southeast of Italy in the summer of 205. According to the Roman historian Livy (28.46.16), it provided a record of his *res gestae* or achievements, perhaps not unlike the document of that name which was promulgated after the death of the Emperor Augustus in AD 14 in commemoration of his Principate. A Latin inscription from Brindisi commemorating the capture of Tarentum by Quintus Fabius Maximus contains the only surviving contemporary mention of Hannibal by name. The archaeological record is confined to the remains of camps and fortifications that are contemporary with Hannibal and sheds very little light on our subject. Though grave pits have been discovered close to the site of Hannibal's victory at Lake Trasimene in 217, there is no scholarly consensus as to whether they relate to the battle.

It is also worth noting that we do not have any idea of the response to Hannibal's campaign on the part of his countrymen, nor do we know how they viewed him at later moments during his life, after the

Battle of Zama, or after he had fled into exile, or after he had committed suicide. Were Carthaginian children encouraged to revere him as a shining example of Punic hardihood and pluck that all but broke the might of Rome, or as a wayward and undisciplined adventurer who was consumed by a fatally destructive lust for power?

At least three Greeks and one Roman wrote contemporary accounts of Hannibal's campaign that have not survived. Two of the Greeks were in his retinue – a Sicilian called Silenus from the Cretan coastal town of Cale Akte, and the Spartan Sosylus. The later Greek historian Polybius dismisses the accounts of both Sosylus and of the third, an otherwise unknown Chaereas, as 'the kind of common gossip that one hears in a barber's shop' (3.20.5). There's no way of knowing whether his opinion is justified or whether he's being purely malicious, but the accounts of Silenus and Sosylus would obviously have been favourable to their patron, and it may be that Polybius, who was distinctly pro-Roman (see below), allowed this fact to colour his judgement. Hannibal probably took Silenus and Sosylus with him to Italy to record his deeds for the edification of his compatriots back home, members of the Senate especially, just as Alexander the Great took the historian Callisthenes with him on his expedition to Persia with the purpose of sending back dispatches to mainland Greece from the front. But he would also have been keen to present his campaign in the best possible light to Greek speakers, particularly to those Greeks who inhabited southern Italy and Sicily. We do not know where the narrative of either Silenus or Sosylus broke off, but it is highly improbable that Hannibal would have wanted them to write about his defeat at Zama. (The last attested event covered by Silenus dates to 209.)

The contemporary account from the Roman side was by a prominent senator named Quintus Fabius Pictor, who fought in the Second Punic War. His history, written in Greek, began with the foundation of Rome and extended at least as far as the Battle of Lake

31

Trasimene, if not to the end of the war. It has survived only in fragments and none of them sheds much light on Hannibal himself. Pictor wrote in Greek both for Greeks and for educated Romans who could read Greek. It has been argued, with some plausibility, that one of the reasons for this was that he wanted to provide a counterweight to the influence of Silenus and Sosylus. Both Polybius and the Roman historian Livy used Fabius' work, though Livy may have known of it only second-hand.

Other Roman historians who wrote about the Second Punic War include Lucius Cincius Alimentus, praetor of Sicily in 210/209, who was taken prisoner by Hannibal; Cato the Elder (234-149), who was the first Roman to write a history in Latin; and Gaius Acilius (*fl.* 155), whose history, written in Greek, is known to have included an account of the Battle of Cannae (Cicero, *On Duties* 3.115). Alimentus is a particularly interesting figure, as he conversed with Hannibal and was treated by him with respect (Livy 21.38.2-5). He was therefore privy to the Carthaginian perspective on the war.

Our most reliable source, as well as our earliest extant one, is that of Polybius (*c.* 200-*c.* 118). Polybius, who was Hannibal's younger contemporary by about 20 years, tells us that he set it as his task to explain 'how and with what sort of constitution almost the whole of the known world was conquered and came under the rule of the Romans in less than 53 years' (1.1.5), that is, from just before the outbreak of the Second Punic War to the end of Macedonian independence in 167. The phrase 'almost the whole of the known world' lends a certain grandeur to his topic. What he actually means is 'almost the whole western Mediterranean'. Of the original 40 books he wrote, only the first five survive intact. His account of the Second Punic War, which begins in Book 3, becomes fragmentary after the Battle of Cannae in 216. We also have a large part of Book 6, in which Polybius admiringly sets out the qualities of the Roman constitution that enabled it to surmount the challenge that Hannibal posed. We have only fragments of the remaining 34 books, though we are fortunate to have his account of the Battle of Zama in Book 15.

True, Polybius has two strikes against him: he was fervently pro-Roman, and he was a client (i.e. a dependant in the technical Roman sense) of the Scipios, the family that produced Publius Cornelius Scipio Aemilianus, who was later given the *agnomen* or honorific title 'Africanus' in honour of his victory over Hannibal in Africa. The two facts are obviously related. His patron, who was probably about twenty years younger than he, was Publius Cornelius Scipio Aemilianus (later also earning the title 'Africanus'), adopted grandson of the Scipio referred to above. Polybius was one of 1,000 prominent Greeks from Achaea, a region in the northeast Peloponnese, who were summoned to Rome in 167 to undergo interrogation concerning their conduct in the war that the Romans had just won against Perseus, king of Macedonia. He remained in Rome under house arrest until 151. Like Fabius Pictor, Polybius wrote in Greek, both for Greeks and for Romans who knew Greek. He is a unique phenomenon in the history of Greek historiography, as he was a committed advocate of Roman supremacy in the Mediterranean.

But these concerns aside, Polybius deserves our respect for a number of reasons. To begin with, he was anything but an armchair historian, and his accounts of military operations are among the best to come down to us from classical antiquity. He even attempted to retrace Hannibal's route through the Alps, though what he learnt by doing this is unclear (3.48.12). Hannibal obviously fascinated him and his historical 'tourism' should be seen as an act of homage. Secondly, Polybius interviewed both 'the men who happened to be present at the time' and 'eyewitnesses', including, probably, Carthaginians who had fought in the war (3.48.12; cf. 4.2.2). During his time in Rome he may well have questioned Roman veterans as well, many of whom would have been only too ready to talk about their experiences. Oral evidence was one of his principal sources, though this is likely to have been somewhat partial and inaccurate, not least because Polybius was probably born shortly after the end of the Second Punic War, so his 'witnesses' would have been very old by the time he began interrogating them (12.4c.2-5). Even so, it is commendable that he deemed the exercise worthwhile. A third point in Polybius' favour is that he consulted documents in Rome's archives describing its dealings with Carthage, including copies of all the treaties between the two sides (e.g. 3.22-8). He also inspected the inscription set up by Hannibal at Cape Colonna, which he quoted first as his source for the size and composition of Hannibal's army before it set out for Spain, second for the length of time it took Hannibal to march from Spain to Italy, and third for the size of his army when he descended into Italy (3.33.18; 3.56.1-4).

Our most important Roman source is Livy (59 BC-AD 17), who wrote a history of Rome in 142 books from its foundation to 9 BC. Only 35 of these books have survived complete, but they include Books 21-30, which deal with the Second Punic War, and Books 31-5, which describe Hannibal's fortunes after his defeat at Zama. The fact that these particular books have survived is a measure of their popularity in antiquity and of the continuing interest in Hannibal. Despite the fact that he is intensely patriotic, Livy presents him sympathetically. Not only did he find much to admire, but he also remained interested in his fortunes after he had been driven into exile. His ambivalence was no doubt shared by many of his readers.

We know very little about Livy's life, other than the fact that he was hired by Augustus to tutor the future emperor Claudius. Since he was neither a soldier nor a politician, he lacked the qualifications for writing history that Polybius so prized. He relied heavily on his predecessor, so much so that in some places, as in his description of Hannibal crossing the Alps, he can fairly be accused of plagiarising him, even though he sometimes mistranslates him. Yet despite his dependence, he mentions Polybius only once by name (30.45.5). Though Livy is writing over a century and a half after the end of the war, we have no alternative but to rely on his account for the period from 216 onwards when Polybius' narrative breaks off.

Though Livy had his shortcomings, he was not wholly deficient in critical acumen. He seems to have owned copies of all the surviving accounts of the Second Punic War that he could lay his hands on, or perhaps of summaries thereof, and at times he makes a valiant effort to assess their credibility. In this respect he comes closest of all ancient historians to anticipating the modern historiographical practice of *Quellenforschung* or source criticism. The historians he cites include Fabius Pictor, Lucius Coelius Antipater (late second century BC), Valerius Antias, and Claudius Quadrigarius (both first century BC). Livy references them whenever he encounters disagreements in their accounts. Examples include the route that Hannibal took over the Alps, the size of his army on his arrival in Italy, and the route that he took to Rome in 211. Sometimes, too, he invokes popular tradition ('men say', meaning 'Romans say') as his authority. Occasionally his patience runs out and on one occasion this provokes him to declare, 'There is no end to the lies that historians tell.'

Hannibal features in a number of other historical accounts. Diodorus Siculus (*c.* 80-*c.* 29 BC) is the author of a *Historical Library* in Greek in 40 books which runs from mythological times up to 60 BC. It is particularly important for our understanding of events in Sicily, which are preserved in the extant portions of Books 25-7. Pompeius Trogus, a Romanised Gaul who probably lived in the reign of Augustus, wrote a lost work called the *Philippic Histories*, which included some information about Hannibal's later years. It survives in an epitome (or abridgement) by Justin, an author who is variously assigned to the second, third or even fourth century AD. Appian of Alexandria (AD *c.* 95-*c.* 165) wrote a *Roman History* in Greek in 24 books, which includes an account of the Second Punic War divided into *Hannibalica*, *Punica*, *Iberica* and *Libyca*. Appian is often inaccurate and unreliable when he can be measured against other sources. However, he also includes material that is exclusive to his account that should not automatically be dismissed. And he at least attempts to provide an even-handed assessment of Hannibal, castigating him at times for his cruelty, while lauding him for his achievements. Finally, Eutropius, who served under the Emperor Julian in his campaign against the Persians in AD 363, wrote a *breviarium* or survey of Roman history in ten books. Book 3 offers an account of the Second Punic War, mainly drawn from the epitome of Livy.

What is sadly lacking is any biography worthy of the name. Cornelius Nepos (*c.* 110-24 BC), Rome's first extant biographer, wrote a very abbreviated account. He also wrote an even more abbreviated biography of Hannibal's father Hamilcar. None the less he drew from sources that are favourable to Hannibal and he provided an outline of his career after his defeat at Zama. Regrettably antiquity's greatest biographer, Plutarch (born before AD 50; died after AD 120), who wrote parallel lives of Greeks and Romans, did not attempt a biography of Hannibal. One can only speculate as to whom he might have paired him with, either Greek or Roman. He did, however, write biographies of both Quintus Fabius Maximus, the famous 'Delayer' who was appointed dictator after Rome's defeat at Cannae, and of Marcus Claudius Marcellus, who captured Syracuse from the Carthaginians. These shed considerable light upon events during the Second Punic War, even though Hannibal features only incidentally in both.

Even in antiquity historians were fascinated to know the route that Hannibal took across the Alps. They include Polybius, Livy, the Roman antiquarian Marcus Terentius Varro, the Greek historian Timagenes of Alexandria, and the Greek geographer Strabo.[1]

---

[1] J.F. Lazenby, *Hannibal's War* (Aris & Phillips 1978) Appendix I provides a full list of all the surviving written sources.

2. The Witnesses

Winston Churchill once said, 'History will be kind to me for I intend to write it.' Though Hannibal had done as much as anyone could in those days to ensure that the memory of his achievements would not be preserved solely in the Roman historiographical tradition, it is highly likely that the writings of the two men who actually accompanied him on the campaign and who 'remained with him as long as fortune permitted' (Nepos, *Hannibal* 13.3), namely Silenus and Sosylus, had disappeared by the first century AD. We thus observe him through a glass darkly.

3

The Carthaginian State

Carthage, a city inhabited by a people we call today the Phoenicians, was in Hannibal's day a thriving port situated on a large peninsula at the most northerly projecting tip of the African coastline in the Bay of Tunis. Today its remains are located in a suburb of Tunis of the same name. At its height, before the outbreak of the First Punic War in 264 BC, it was arguably the most important trading community in the Mediterranean. Its wealth derived from its location, its excellent harbour facilities, and its fertile hinterland. It first rose to prominence in the seventh century BC by bringing other Phoenician settlements in the western Mediterranean under its sway. As Polybius (3.38.2) notes, in time it came to control 'all the coastline of Africa from the Altars of Philaenus (the ancient boundary between Egypt and Cyrene on the Gulf of Sidra) and the Pillars of Hercules (the Straits of Gibraltar)'. That is to say, its direct politico-military power extended eastwards to include the coastal strips of Tripolitanian (i.e. western) Libya and Tunisia, and westwards to include the coastal strips of Morocco and Algeria. What we do not know is how far inland Carthage's control extended. At its height it also controlled Sardinia, western Sicily, Malta, southern Spain, and the Balearic Islands. (The Balearic Islands derive their name from *ballein*, the Greek verb meaning 'to throw', owing to the skill of the islanders in the use of the slingshot. Balearic archers, who used special composite bows, would constitute an important contingent in Hannibal's invasion force.) Punic culture and the Punic language spread throughout this whole region, and they remained dominant forces there for about a century after Carthage's destruction in 146 BC.

The first excavations in Carthage were undertaken in 1857 by a French archaeologist and politician called Charles Ernest Beulé, who published his findings in *Fouilles à Carthage* in 1861. Most of what has come to light dates to the period after the city had been re-founded as a Roman colony by the Emperor Augustus. However, a striking discovery was made in 1921 when archaeologists came upon a religious sanctuary packed with thousands of vases containing the charred bones of newborn children, thought to be associated with human sacrifice (see further below). Though a large number of Punic inscriptions have been found within the city environs, they have shed little light upon Carthaginian culture, since most of them are funerary and highly formulaic.

Until the outbreak of the First Punic War, relations between Carthage and Rome were extremely cordial, as evidenced by a series of treaties between the two states, the most recent of which was concluded in 279. In 264, however, the Romans invaded Sicily, then a Carthaginian protectorate, in support of mercenaries from Campania called the Mamertines, who controlled Messana (modern Messina). When the Romans, after relieving Messana, went on to subjugate Syracuse, the Carthaginians became alarmed and sent a force to Sicily. The Romans faced an uphill battle at the outset of the war as they lacked a proper navy. In 260, however, they built a fleet of 200 quinqueremes and 20 triremes. The quinquereme, which was destined to become the principal Roman warship, was perhaps so named because it was rowed by oarsmen who sat in groups of five. Interestingly its design was modelled on a captured Carthaginian warship (Polybius 1.20.15 and 59.8). Though the Romans managed to land an invasion force in Africa as early as 256, the First Punic War dragged on until 241, when the Carthaginians finally sued for peace. The Romans imposed very harsh terms, requiring them to evacuate

Sicily and pay an indemnity of 3,200 talents over ten years. In 238 they annexed Sardinia and imposed a further indemnity.

We should by no means think of the two as mortal enemies, however. Even after Carthage's defeat in the Second Punic War, they continued to have commercial dealings. Plautus' comic play *Poenulus* ('The Little Phoenician'), which was produced in 190, indicates that the Romans were extremely familiar with Carthaginian traders. Though the little Phoenician of the title, a merchant named Hanno, is a stock character who speaks gibberish (somewhat similar to the type we encounter in the comedies of Aristophanes), he has several redeeming features, including a deep affection for his daughters, and there is no evidence of any animus towards him on Plautus' part. This is interesting in light of the fact that the historians, who wrote for the élite, do reveal racial bias against the Carthaginians.

The Phoenicians, a Semitic-speaking people, arrived in the region that we call Phoenicia (a coastal strip in the Levant about 200 miles in length stretching from modern Syria in the north to Galilee in the south) some time in the second millennium BC. Because they could not support themselves by agriculture alone, they engaged in maritime trade, at which they excelled. Among their principal exports was Tyrian crimson (named after the city of Tyre), a highly prized dye made from the mucus of a sea snail known as *murex trunculus*. It may have been this dye that gave the Phoenicians their Greek name *Phoinikes*, which derives from the adjective *phoinios*, meaning 'purple' or 'red'. Another possible explanation is that 'red' refers to the colour of their skin. The Romans took over the name *Phoinikes* and transcribed it as *Poeni*. Hence our word 'Punic', which comes from the adjective *poenicus*. What the Phoenicians called themselves is a mystery – if indeed they called themselves anything or thought of themselves as a single ethnic entity. They may simply have referred to themselves as Carthaginians, Sidonians, Tyrians, etc. Another important Phoenician export was the vowel-less alphabet, which the Greeks in the eighth century adapted to their language by adding seven vowel sounds to the original sixteen Phoenician consonants. Many of the Phoenician names for their letters entered the Greek alphabet, including *aleph* (alpha), meaning 'ox-head' and *beth* (beta), meaning 'house'.

Phoenicia was not a state as such. Rather it was a collection of city kingdoms, chief among which were Sidon, Tyre and Byblos (Phoenician Gebal, Arabic Jbeil). Byblos was so named by the Greeks because it was via this city that they imported papyrus from Egypt, hence our word 'Bible'. It is one of the oldest cities in the world. According to Herodotus (2.44.3) the Phoenicians migrated from the Persian Gulf 2,300 years before his time, i.e. in 2800 BC. They all spoke the same language, worshipped the same gods, and adhered to common institutions, though they remained politically independent from one another. In other words, Phoenician cities operated very much on the lines of Greek city-states or *poleis*, which also jealously guarded their freedom, notwithstanding having a language, a system of religious belief, and social and political institutions in common. From the eleventh century onwards, in line with the expansion of the population of Phoenicia, these cities established trading posts and in some cases agricultural communities abroad, the most important being Carthage, rather in the same way that Greek city-states sent out colonies under the pressure of an expanding population. This movement reached its height in the ninth and eighth centuries BC. In the sixth century BC Phoenicia was overrun by the Persians and two centuries later by Alexander the Great. Carthage and its neighbour Utica, however, continued to flourish as independent communities.

According to tradition, Carthage was founded in 814 BC, though the earliest pottery does not pre-date the second half of the eighth century BC. Its name in Phoenician is *Qart Hadasht*, which means 'New Town'. The Greeks called it *Karkhêdôn*, the Romans Carthago. It owed its name to the fact that it was new in relation to Utica (*Atiq* in Carthaginian), which lay on the coast about 18 miles to the north (see the map on p. 110). Utica had allegedly been founded in 1101 BC, though its earliest pottery is of eighth-century date. Carthage was supposedly founded by Dido (Phoenician name Elissa), the sister of Pygmalion, king of Tyre. According to legend Dido married her uncle Sychaeus, by no means an uncommon occurrence in antiquity. When Pygmalion had her husband murdered, Dido escaped with her companions to Libya, where she struck a deal with a local king called Iarbas. Iarbas agreed to let her establish as large a kingdom as she could cover with an ox-hide. To maximise upon the deal, she cut the ox-hide into the thinnest of thin strips, thereby establishing a reputation for Punic deviousness, which also attached to Hannibal. Several different versions of the Dido story existed until Virgil in the late first century BC established the definitive one from a Roman (i.e. Augustan) perspective with his description of her ill-fated affair with Aeneas in Book 4 of the *Aeneid*. Since Dido curses Aeneas and his descendants when he abandons her, the poem provides a religious as well as historical explanation for Hannibal's deep-rooted hatred of the Romans.

It is entirely possible that the population of the Carthaginian state was comparable in size to that of the Roman Republic, though it certainly did not possess the same reserves of manpower. The Roman Republic comprised the Latin colonies plus a number of subjugated states in the Italian peninsula that were allied to Rome. These Latin colonies, whose inhabitants were citizens of independent states, were expected to protect Roman interests in the region. They extended from the Po Valley in the north (e.g. Cremona and Placentia, founded as recently as 220 BC) to the heel of Italy (e.g. Brundisium, modern Brindisi, on the Adriatic coast). The actual citizen body of Carthage was minute by comparison because the Carthaginians did not extend citizenship to their conquered peoples.

Very likely Carthage's population, though predominantly Semitic-speaking, was racially mixed. We know that Hannibal married a

Spaniard and that two of his sisters married Numidians, and what was common in terms of marriage patterns at the top of the social scale was probably equally common at the bottom. The Numidians were a nomadic people who lived inland from Carthage and to the west, nominally independent but within Carthage's sphere of influence. At the time of the Second Punic War there were two tribal confederacies, the Masaesylii under king Syphax to the west, and the Massyli under king Masinissa to the east. Both confederacies played an important part in the war.

The most important Carthaginian deity was Ba'al Hammon, a somewhat shadowy figure whose worship in the region preceded the arrival of the Phoenicians. Some scholars associate Ba'al Hammon etymologically with the Greek god Zeus Ammon, who was worshipped both in the city of Cyrene (modern Shahat in Libya) and at the oasis of Siwa in Egypt's western desert. Another theory is that Hammon derives from Semitic *hmm*, meaning fire, in which case Ba'al Hammon might be taken to mean 'lord of the fires', a possible reference to sacrifice by immolation. Ba'al is thought to have been in charge of fertility and is associated with the Greek god Kronos, whom the Romans identified with Saturn. No less shadowy was Carthage's principal female deity Tanit. Tanit is thought to have been connected with Astarte (Hebrew Ashtoreth, Mesopotamian Ishtar), a goddess of war, fertility and sexuality, whom the Greeks identified with Aphrodite. Another important deity was Melqart (the name means 'king of the city'). The Greeks identified Melqart with Herakles (Roman Hercules), the greatest of their heroes, whom they elevated to the rank of an Olympian god. To secure Melqart's goodwill, Hannibal visited his shrine at Gades (Cádiz) before setting off on his campaign.

What marks this belief system out from most other contemporary Mediterranean religions is the practice of child-sacrifice, which Plato describes as 'holy and in accordance with the law' in Carthaginian eyes (*Minos* 315bc). The Greek historian Diodorus Siculus (20.14.5-6) claims that when Agathocles, tyrant of Syracuse, made an assault upon the city in 310 BC, 200 Carthaginian children of aristocratic birth were placed in the arms of a bronze statue of Kronos (i.e. Ba'al Hammon), which then pitched them into a pit of fire. Though archaeologists have failed to come up with any data to corroborate the existence of Diodorus' fanciful automaton, recent excavations conducted by Serge Lancel (*Carthage: A History* [Oxford 1995] 227-56) for the American School of Oriental Research have provided evidence for child sacrifice in the fourth and third centuries BC. This is indicated by the discovery of a number of urns containing the cremated remains of children aged mainly between one and three, which had been buried in an open-air sacrificial area customarily referred to as a 'tophet'. What is striking about many of the urns is that they contain the remains of two or even three children, which suggests that the children belonged to the same family and met their deaths at the same time. Archaeological evidence for the custom dies out around the end of the first century BC, perhaps because of Roman opposition to human sacrifice, though the Church father Tertullian, himself a native of Carthage, claims that it actually continued under Roman domination (*Apology* 9.2-3). With what frequency the Carthaginians practised human sacrifice at the time of the Second Punic War is unknown.

We see Carthage, as we see Hannibal, exclusively through Greek and Roman eyes. This is deeply problematic as the Roman élite had little respect and less sympathy for the Carthaginian people. As Norman Davies (*Europe* [Oxford 1996] 108) has pointedly suggested, their story has very likely suffered in the record from 'yet another variant of antisemitism'. Reconstructing Carthage's constitution in detail is an impossible undertaking. Superficially it resembled that of Republican Rome, though there is no evidence that it owed anything to it. We know little about how Carthage administered its empire and next to nothing about its social structure. The Emperor

Claudius wrote eight books of Carthaginian history but no trace of them has survived (Suetonius, *Claudius* 42.2).

Aristotle (*Politics* 1272b24-1273b26), writing a century before Hannibal's birth, compared Carthage's constitution to that of Sparta and Crete. He ignores Rome, and Carthage is in fact the only non-Greek state he discusses. Aristotle approved of the fact that it exhibited a 'mixed constitution', i.e. one which contained the best elements of the three chief political systems known to the ancient world: monarchy, oligarchy and democracy. These elements were represented respectively by the king, the Council of Elders and the Assembly. We do not know whether the Assembly comprised all the male citizens or whether those at the bottom of the economic heap were excluded. From a democratic perspective Aristotle greatly deplored the fact that preference was given to wealth over what he calls *aretê* or virtue in electing public officers, since this meant that 'the whole state was money-grubbing'. Polybius also saw much to admire in the Carthaginian state, which he compared to both Sparta and Rome.

Aristotle makes no mention of the chief magistracy at the time of the Punic Wars, namely the suffetate, which was known at least in Tyre in the fifth century BC. The Latin term for this office is *suffes* (alternative spelling *sufes*), which is a transliteration of *shophet* or *shouphet*, the Punic word for 'judge'. *Suffetes* seem to have been elected primarily on the basis of birth and wealth. Pompeius Trogus (in the epitome of Justin 31.2.6) uses the word 'consul' to describe Hannibal in his role as *suffes*, though we should note that *suffetes*, unlike consuls, did not hold military or naval commands, which were held by separately elected generals. Greek historians rarely transliterate the word *suffes*, though it is likely that the word *basileus*, meaning 'king', denotes this office in their accounts. They may have believed that the magistracy evolved from the kingship, as happened in Athens, where *basileus* described the senior ranking magistrate, who took

45

over some of the functions previously invested in the king. Aristotle actually equated the *suffetes* with the Spartan *basileis*.

Carthaginian magistrates served for only one year; the Senate, which was otherwise known as 'The Mighty Ones', was composed of ex-magistrates; and the primary task of the Assembly was to elect officials and ratify laws, all of which features were equally true of the Roman Republic. The Carthaginian constitution was not, however, a copy of its Roman counterpart. On the contrary, inscriptions suggest that it predated the Roman by nearly a century. Though Polybius claims that 'in Carthage the voice of the people became predominant in deliberations' (6.51), the Assembly was overshadowed by the Senate, especially in matters having to do with the conduct of war, and important decisions were sometimes taken without seeking its approval. It is important to note, however, that Hannibal's election to the post of general was ratified by a unanimous vote of the people (Polybius 3.13.4). There was also an inner Council of Thirty and a court consisting of 104 judges which Aristotle refers to as the Hundred. In effect Carthage was a narrow oligarchy.

Whereas Rome's generals normally were appointed annually, Carthage seems to have appointed its generals for the entire duration of a campaign. They thus had far more independence than their Roman counterparts. This led to tensions with the Senate when a campaign became protracted, as during the Second Punic War. It also meant that the Roman demand that the Senate hand over Hannibal after the destruction of Saguntum was unrealistic. Some scholars have compared Hannibal in his capacity as general to a ruler of a semi-independent kingdom on the march. Since it was Carthaginian practice to crucify its unsuccessful generals, this semi-independence came at a very high price, though Hannibal himself did not suffer this fate.

Rome's army consisted mainly of citizen farmers supplemented by an approximately equal number of allies. By contrast, the core of

3. The Carthaginian State

Carthage's fighting force comprised subject peoples and mercenaries. Most of its soldiers were either Libyans, Numidians or Iberians. The Libyans were not permitted to raise their own forces but required to serve in the Carthaginian army. They also had to render more than a quarter of their produce to the Carthaginians. The Numidians, who made up the bulk of the Carthaginian cavalry, were a more privileged ethnic entity than the Libyans and as a result did not have to pay tribute. The Iberians (i.e. Spanish) were required to provide troops and, probably, pay tribute.

On the Roman side by contrast, all male citizens above a minimum property qualification aged between 17 and 46 were liable for military service. Each legion (the word means 'selection') consisted of 4,500-5,000 legionaries divided into ten cohorts. A consular army comprised two Roman legions and two allied legions, since Rome required its allies to supply an equal number of troops. The estimated number of soldiers available at the time of the Second Punic War, inclusive of the allies, is half a million. Though the city never mobilised anything like its total available manpower, its ultimate victory was largely due to the fact that even in its darkest hours it had reserves to draw upon, which was especially important after the devastating defeat at Cannae.

We know precious little about the manner of fighting and organisation of the Carthaginian army. We do not even know whether its infantry relied mainly on swords or on spears. A prominent feature of the Carthaginian army was, of course, its African elephants, which had been used against the Romans in the First Punic War. It is clear that the command structure of the Carthaginian army was more autocratic than its Roman counterpart. Had the situation been different Hannibal would never have been able to employ the audacious, high-risk strategy that was the hallmark of the opening years of his campaign in Italy. We know, too, that he had a number of very able lieutenants, upon whom he placed considerable reliance, though we know little about their respective ranking. They include his brother Mago, his nephew Hanno, and three cavalry commanders called Carthalo, Hasdrubal and Maharbal.

It may seem somewhat surprising that Carthage's navy played so little part in the war, given the city's distinguished maritime tradition and the importance of its navy during the First Punic War. The fact is, however, that on the eve of the outbreak of war it had only 87 warships, compared with 220 Roman warships, and though there were 130 ships off the shores of Sicily in 212, they never won a single victory. Only twice, moreover, did the Carthaginian navy succeed in getting supplies across to Italy – in 215 and 205. Its lack of involvement in the war contributed greatly to Hannibal's failure.

The leading Carthaginian family in the third century was the Barcids. 'Barca' was actually the nickname of Hannibal's father Hamilcar, but modern scholars have assigned the name Barcid to all the family members. According to Virgil, Hamilcar was descended from Dido's father, Belus (*Aeneid* 1.621, 729), though Silius Italicus makes Belus one of the men who accompanied Dido when she fled from Tyre (*Punic War* 1.71-3). We do not know how the Barcids came to prominence, but they probably made their money from trade, like most wealthy Carthaginians. Just as the Barcids were in the business of breaking the might of Rome, so on the Roman side the Scipionic family, first Publius Cornelius Scipio and his younger brother Gnaeus, and then, a generation later, Publius' son, who bore the same name as his father, was in the business of destroying their aspirations. Hannibal's story is therefore in part a story about two families locked in deadly conflict. Despite his pre-eminence and enterprise, however, Hannibal was deeply resented by non-Barcid aristocrats. This resentment was probably responsible for the diffident support the Carthaginian Senate provided to him as the Italian campaign lengthened. It certainly surfaced with a vengeance from 203 onwards, once the campaign was lost, and it was the reason behind his eventual exile in 195.

3. The Carthaginian State

In 146 the Romans destroyed Carthage, though they did not, as has been alleged, raze it to the ground (see further p. 131f.). What makes this act more shocking is that they did so after the city had offered to surrender. The site, under a curse, remained unoccupied for a century. Then in 44 Julius Caesar introduced a plan to re-found it as *Colonia Iulia Carthago*, though this was not implemented until after his death by Octavian. Perhaps as early as 40 or 39 it became the capital of the Roman province of Africa (*Africa nova*). The city continued to expand and reached its pinnacle of prosperity under the dynasty established by the 'African' emperor Septimius Severus, who came to the throne in AD 193. However, it has hardly fared much better than its predecessor in terms of archaeological remains. In fact the site today is barely worth a stop on the tourist itinerary, though the Bardo Museum, which contains many important Carthaginian and Roman finds, most certainly is. The Romans and modern development have done their stuff. Since 1972 UNESCO, with the co-operation of the Tunisian Institut National d'Archéologie et d'Art, has funded a campaign which has greatly increased our knowledge of the city, thanks in part to the work of the British Mission under Henry Hurst of Cambridge University. Its principal focus has, however, been the later history of the site, and few traces of Hannibal's Carthage have come to light.

4

The Spanish Command

Nothing is known of Hannibal's early childhood, other than the fact that he grew up in the shadow of Carthage's defeat in the First Punic War. He was five or six when the war ended and was no doubt deeply affected, like others of his generation, by the humiliating terms of the peace, just as Hitler was haunted by the similarly humiliating terms that the Treaty of Versailles imposed upon Germany after the First World War. Lacking as we do a Plutarch to chronicle his most formative experiences, we do not know what else might have forged his character other than the example of his father, but the oath of eternal enmity to Rome, if historical, was no doubt critical. Even without it, it is natural, given his family's prominence in Carthaginian society, that he would have been strongly motivated by a desire for vengeance. Hamilcar was convinced that there could be no peaceful co-existence with Rome. Rome's demand at the end of the First Punic War in 241 that the Carthaginians evacuate Sicily, the far western part of which they had colonized, demonstrated the truth of this. Rome's seizure of Sardinia in 238 had further confirmed it. This bitter lesson in *Machtpolitik* the father taught his son.

We cannot be sure but it may have been with the intention of eventually invading Italy that Hamilcar began to develop Spain as a basis for Carthaginian power (Livy 21.2.1-2). He exacted tribute from the native Iberian population and began mining for mineral deposits. He also built up a powerful army comprising both Libyans and Iberians. Hannibal, who, as we've seen, accompanied his father

CARTHAGINIAN SPAIN

to Spain aged nine or ten, must have been fed a stolid diet of anti-Roman propaganda. He was about seventeen when his father was killed in battle in the winter of 229 or 228. We do not know whether at this point he returned to Carthage, even for a brief interval. Hamilcar's son-in-law Hasdrubal (known as 'The Fair'), who succeeded to the command, adopted the same policy as his predecessor, making it his task to extend Carthaginian influence as far north as the River Tagus in central Spain. He did so not only by military action but also by building diplomatic ties with the local chieftains and increasing the size of his army by recruiting Iberians. It was Hasdrubal who in 228 founded the city the Romans called Carthago Nova or New Carthage (modern Cartagena). The Carthaginians called it simply *Qart Hadasht* – the same name as Carthage itself. The city was situated on a peninsula in Murcia overlooking a fine harbour and located close to silver mines. It later became the headquarters for Hannibal's military operations in Spain.

Alerted to the fact that Carthage was extending its grip on Spain, the Romans sent a delegation to Hasdrubal to negotiate a settlement. They wanted to establish what we would call today a sphere of

51

influence. In 226 the two sides reached an agreement by which the River Ebro became the northern boundary of Carthaginian influence. Though the treaty did not explicitly refer to Roman influence, the evident assumption was that the river marked its southern limit since the Carthaginians were forbidden 'to cross the Ebro bearing arms'. The problem with this arrangement was that an Iberian city named Saguntum (modern Sagunto), whose population according to Polybius had placed themselves under the protection of Rome 'a good many years before the time of Hannibal' (3.30.1), lay about 90 miles south of the Ebro, 16 miles north of the modern city of Valencia. It was only a matter of time before the interests of Saguntum would provide a pretext for Roman involvement south of the Ebro – an inevitability that Hasdrubal must have foreseen and perhaps desired. Livy claimed that a clause had been inserted in the settlement guaranteeing the freedom of Saguntum, but this is likely to have been done *post eventum* to justify subsequent Roman action on behalf of the city (21.2.7). Polybius, who consulted the Roman archives, says nothing about Saguntum in his discussion of the treaty.

In 221 Hasdrubal lost his life to an assassin and the army enthusiastically proclaimed Hannibal as its *stratêgos* (in Polybius' Greek) or *dux* (in Livy's Latin). Both words roughly mean commander-in-chief. He was 25 or 26 years old. Polybius reports that when this news reached the Carthaginian Senate an assembly was called, which 'unanimously ratified the army's choice' (3.13.4). Livy tells us that 'from the day he was proclaimed commander-in-chief Hannibal maintained the belief that there should be no delay, as if Italy had been assigned to him as his sphere of power or province (*provincia*) and as if he had been instructed to declare war on Rome' (21.5.1-2). Livy's use of the word *provincia* would have made Roman hackles rise, as in his day this was the technical term either for a territory that had been subjugated by the Romans and was now under Roman administration, or alternatively for one that had been earmarked for subjugation. However, his claim that Hannibal 'from the day he was proclaimed commander-in-chief' was determined to attack Rome rests on very shaky foundations. More likely Hannibal chose his moment to provoke Rome only when he sensed that elements hostile to him in the Carthaginian Senate might be threatening to strip him of his military command, which happened about a year or so later. In the meantime he adopted his father's policy of strengthening Carthage's grip on Spain with a view to securing its immense mineral resources and manpower.

Hannibal spent just two brief years as commander of Carthaginian forces in Spain. His first military action was to lay siege to Althaea, the chief city of a tribe known as the Olcades (see map on p. 51). Althaea lay to the south of the Ebro in the region known today as La Mancha. At the end of his first campaigning season he returned to his winter quarters in Carthago Nova. The following year he extended his operations further north into the territory of the Vaccaei (around the borders of Leon and Old Castile) and the Carpetani (in the Sierra di Guadarrama, north of the River Tagus). He succeeded in subduing most of the Iberian peninsula south of the Ebro, with the notable exception of the town of Saguntum, which he left alone.

The defining moment in Hannibal's life occurred in the winter of 220/219. Some time previously a conflict had arisen between the Saguntines and a neighbouring tribe allied to Carthage. Livy identifies the people as the Turdetani, but this is unlikely since they lived a great distance from Saguntum. In the spring of 219 Hannibal made a surprise attack on Saguntum. His force is said to have amounted to 150,000 (Livy 21.8.3). Though this figure is likely to be greatly exaggerated, his army may well have been far larger than the one he later commanded in Italy. At some point the Saguntines appealed to the Romans, though we do not know whether this was before the assault had begun or after. The Romans responded by sending an embassy to Spain. The siege of Saguntum was underway when they arrived and Hannibal refused to grant the ambassadors audience. Instead he accused the Romans of having arbitrarily executed some leading Saguntines. Polybius, who records the curt exchange that took place between the two sides, is highly critical of Hannibal, claiming that he let his anger get the better of him (3.15.9). Whether this is a true reading of events or not, the die was cast, since by antagonising the Romans Hannibal had set himself on a path of confrontation that would lead directly to the outbreak of war.

Despite the appeal from the Saguntines, the Romans took no military action. They may have believed that Hannibal had attacked Saguntum without obtaining the agreement of the Carthaginian Senate and that he would in time be required to desist. They may also have counted on the anti-Barcid faction being willing to hand Hannibal over to them. In this they were sorely deceived. Livy reports that only Hanno, Hannibal's leading opponent, spoke in defence of the Ebro treaty and recommended that Hannibal and his officers be handed over to the Romans, but this may well be pure speculation on his part (21.10). How would he have had access to information about the debate? In sum, we just do not know how much opposition there was in the Senate to Hannibal's action.

The Romans expected the Carthaginians to yield to diplomatic pressure. They had, after all, given in to their threats in the inter-war years. Till recently, however, the Romans had had their hands tied protecting northern Italy against the Gauls and they were no doubt reluctant to engage in fresh hostilities so far from home. In 225 they had defeated a Gallic invasion – described by Polybius as 'the most formidable of all their invasions' (2.31.7) – and had followed this up by conducting a series of campaigns whose object was to extend Roman influence as far north as the River Po, in part by settling colonies in the region. Though the Gauls no longer posed an immediate threat, the Romans remained extremely wary of them. In addition, cities allied to Rome in Illyricum (the region from the head of the Adriatic Sea in the north to Epirus in western Greece in the south) were under attack, and this was seen as the principal theatre of action in 219. Accordingly both consuls for that year were sent out east rather than west.

Despite the size of the Carthaginian army, Saguntum held out for eight months before it eventually fell in the late autumn of 219. It was the savage destruction of the city that earned Hannibal the reputation among the Romans of 'perfidy worse than that of an ordinary Carthaginian, disregard for truth and sanctity, etc.', to quote Livy, largely because he gave the order that no prisoners should be taken (21.14.3). Both Polybius (3.17.7) and Livy suggest that it was the immense quantity of booty which he distributed among his troops that fired them with enthusiasm for his forthcoming Italian campaign. Incidentally, the tradition that Saguntum was associated with the Greek island of Zacynthus because of its similar-sounding name is unfounded, as is the Roman belief that its native Iberian name Arsesaken proved that it was associated with the Italian town of Ardea (Livy 21.7.2), though this latter assumption may well have inflamed Roman sentiment further.

The embassy returned to Rome probably around the same time as news of the fall of Saguntum reached the city. The Romans were completely taken aback. Polybius states that they never expected they would be fighting in Italy against Hannibal, but rather in Spain, using Saguntum as a base for their operations (3.15.13). A debate took place in the Senate in which one side recommended further negotiations, while the other demanded an immediate declaration of war. At the end a motion was put to the vote of the people and the decision was taken to declare war conditionally. A five-man delegation was sent to Carthage under either Marcus Fabius Buteo or Quintus Fabius Maximus – the latter destined to play a pivotal role in the campaign against Hannibal – with the authority to declare war unless Carthage backed down. Even at this point, the Romans were deter-

Fig. 3. 'His Excellency Q. Fabius offering peace or war to the Carthaginian Senate.' Drawing by John Leech from Gilbert Abbott à Beckett, *The Comic History of Rome*, 1852.

mined to explore every possible diplomatic opening. When the delegation arrived in Carthage, its leader pronounced that he held both war and peace in the folds of his toga and that he would let fall whichever they chose. The *suffes* in charge of the Senate meeting asked him which he preferred. 'War,' he announced with the appropriate dramatic flourish of his toga, whereupon the Carthaginians replied without demur, 'We accept' (Polybius 3.33.1-4). It seems that at this point the whole Carthaginian Senate was in accord.

Which brings us to the question: which side was ultimately responsible for the war? The answer was hotly debated in antiquity. Polybius (3.30) argued that, if the sack of Saguntum was the cause of the war, then the Carthaginians were to blame, whereas if the filching of Sardinia and the exaction of tribute was the cause, then the Romans were the guilty party, all the more so because they had led the Carthaginians to believe that in time they would seek to extend their sphere of influence over the entire Iberian peninsula. What then can we say about Hannibal? To what extent should he be held personally responsible? This question, too, was hotly debated in antiquity. Fabius Pictor, for instance, claimed that Hannibal embarked upon the war in the face of opposition from the Carthaginian aristocracy. Polybius, taking issue with Pictor, argued that if the Carthaginians had been opposed to the war they would have handed over Hannibal to the Romans, though that raises the question of how much control they had over him at this point (3.8-9; see also reference to *sunedroi* on p. 20). Overall, however, Polybius is correct in seeking a more broad-based explanation for the outbreak of war than one that lays it solely at the door of one man.

The fact remains that the Romans were ill-prepared for war and would hardly have picked this precise moment to initiate hostilities against the Carthaginians. Livy tells us that when the Senate learned of the fall of Saguntum, it was overcome with grief (*maeror*), pity (*misericordia*), shame (*pudor*), anger (*ira*), and fear (*metus*) – a powerful mixture of emotions (21.16.2). The consequence was that it 'trembled rather than deliberated', as it debated what course of action to follow. This was hardly the mindset of a nation eager to declare war, though we should acknowledge that Livy was seeking to present his countrymen as the injured party. There was nothing unusual in this. The Romans invariably claimed to be the injured party in order to justify initiating hostilities.

Hannibal had made a pre-emptive strike. Expediency and expeditiousness would be the hallmarks of his opening campaign. It is entirely appropriate, therefore, as Polybius points out, that 'the second war between the Romans and Carthaginians became known by most people as the Hannibalic war' (2.37.2).

5

The Epic March

Hannibal was appointed commander not only of the forces in Spain but also of those at home. So while he wintered in Carthago Nova, his first task was to ensure the security of Carthage during his absence. To this end he sent 16,000 men to Africa and raised another 4,000 to defend the capital. Simultaneously, he transferred an almost equal number of soldiers from Africa to Spain. Polybius praises him for sending troops from Spain to Africa and *vice versa*, a course of action which he describes as 'very sensible and wise' (3.33.8), in that it bound the two regions in reciprocal loyalty. He also advised his brother Hasdrubal on how to administer Carthage and resist the Romans if they should launch an attack in his absence. Lastly, he sent messengers to those Gauls who were known to be hostile to Rome, seeking their assistance in the war by giving extravagant promises in return. Securing the support of the Gauls was crucial to his enterprise, in terms of both military assistance and information-gathering, particularly about which route to take over the Alps. Livy tells us that when the Romans likewise sought to elicit support from the Gauls, they were greeted with howls of derision (21.20). This was hardly surprising: the Gauls had sacked Rome in 396 BC and relations were very strained (see above, p. 54). All these tasks would have taken time, and it may be that he did not undertake them until the early spring of 218.

From a tactical point of view Hannibal's decision to invade Italy via the Alps was not as preposterous as it may seem, given the practical difficulties he would have had to face in attempting a naval operation. Carthage's existing fleet was not up to the challenge of taking on the Roman navy, which comprised 220 quinqueremes in 218 (Polybius 3.41.2). In addition, the state, still impoverished from the indemnity it had been ordered to pay at the end of the First Punic War, lacked the resources to build a new fleet. Nor did it have any naval bases in Sicily. Besides which, quite simply, Hannibal seems not to have been a naval man.

In addition, a land invasion had the advantage of making him largely self-reliant, and this probably held considerable appeal for him. He may have suspected that the Senate would be only half-hearted in its support – and so at times it proved. (It had signally failed to provide his father with the necessary resources in Sicily during the First Punic War.) A land invasion would also afford him a better opportunity to rally the Gauls to his cause than would a naval expedition. But though the plan served him well enough in the short term, the absence of a fleet contributed significantly to the failure of his campaign, since, lacking access to a port, he became landlocked and therefore dependent on foraging.

We know very little about the preparations for the march and nothing about the inevitable objections that many in the Carthaginian Senate must have raised. His soldiers were drawn from Carthage, Libya, Numidia, Spain and the Balearic Islands. By far the largest contingent came from Spain, though it is unclear what proportion of his army this contingent represented. Though the Spanish soldiers were mercenaries, this did not mean they were untrustworthy. On the contrary, lacking any sense of national identity, they would have been bound to their paymaster by a very strong bond, and, since they identified his fortunes with their own, would not lightly have broken it, especially since, as foreigners in Italy, they had no other means of livelihood. But how on earth did he get them to accompany him in the first place? Did they actually know what his goal was? Did he suggest it would be a walk in the park? Or did he perhaps intimate that Gaul was the limit of his ambition?

After reviewing 'all the contingents of all the nations', Hannibal visited the Phoenician city of Gadir (Latin, Gades, modern Cádiz), where he 'paid his vows to Herakles-Melqart and bound himself by new ones' (Livy 21.21.9). The journey, some 750 miles roundtrip, must have taken him over a month. It is somewhat reminiscent of the one that Alexander the Great made to Siwa in the Libyan desert in deference to Zeus Ammon during his campaign against Persia, though there's no evidence that Hannibal was imitating Alexander or seeking to put himself on the same footing. Possibly the report of his pilgrimage was inserted into the record later to underscore Hannibal's hatred of Rome and lend credence to the belief that he saw himself undertaking what Moslems would call a *jihad*.

Hannibal left Carthago Nova at the head of his army some time between late April and mid-June. The inscription that he later set up on the Lacinian promontory states that his army comprised 90,000 infantry and 12,000 cavalry. That is undoubtedly an exaggeration but probably not a wild one. Hannibal now commanded the largest and most experienced army in the Mediterranean. Given the logistical challenge of putting such a large force in the field, it is tempting to conclude that either he or his predecessor Hasdrubal had begun planning the campaign years beforehand. As we noted earlier, however, it is by no means evident that the decision to invade Italy preceded the attack on Saguntum.

What has captured the popular and artistic imagination more than anything is the fact that he also had 37 elephants in his train (Appian, *Hannibalic War* 1.4). Though they would have functioned primarily as an assault weapon, they may also have been intended to boost the morale of his troops during the march. After all, if elephants could be expected to survive the crossing of the Alps, then so could men. It is even possible that they were intended

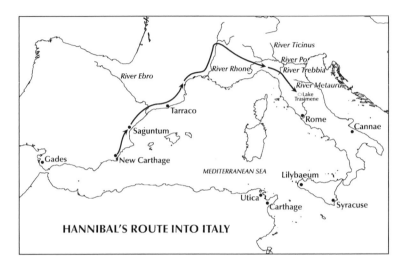

HANNIBAL'S ROUTE INTO ITALY

to be a source of food *en route*, although our sources are silent on this point.

Polybius tells us that Hannibal was in high spirits when he set off, having just learned that the Senate had snubbed the Roman embassy (3.34.7). Taking the coastal route north, he arrived at the Ebro in mid-July, after the flooding that occurred in the spring had subsided. He had now covered about 325 miles. The Greek historian Silenus reported that before crossing the river Hannibal saw a vision of a youth sent by the god Ba'al, who promised to lead him to Italy. Accompanying the youth was a monstrous snake, which seemingly presaged the destruction of Italy (Cicero, *On Divination* 1.49; Livy 21.22.5-9). No doubt Hannibal disseminated this story among his troops to inspire them with the belief that his mission was divinely sanctioned, in much the same way that Julius Caesar later inspired his troops by claiming to have had an epiphany of the goat god Pan when he was crossing the Rubicon. Crossing the Ebro was the decisive act of aggression for Hannibal, just as crossing the Rubicon was for Julius Caesar, since it initiated the Civil War with Pompey: from now on there could be no turning back. Polybius claims that he made rapid progress through northern Spain, though he now had to face attacks from hostile Iberian tribes, eager to prevent their territory from falling into Carthaginian hands (3.35.3). He would also have had to spend some time establishing secure bases in northern Spain to keep his line of communication open once he arrived in Italy.

Hannibal left one of his commanders called Hanno (probably not his nephew of the same name) in charge of the Iberian peninsula north of the Ebro with a force of 10,000 infantry and 1,000 cavalry. So as to be unencumbered when crossing the Alps, he entrusted him with his heavy baggage, intending that it be sent on later. Sensing for the first time the dangers and difficulties that lay ahead, a large number of his men, presumably mercenaries, now deserted his cause. Rather than deal with the demoralising effect of constant desertions, Hannibal dismissed (a further?) 10,000 men, whose loyalty he suspected. By the time he reached the foothills of the Pyrenees in July or August, he had completed nearly half his journey. The worst was yet to come, however, as Polybius reminds us (3.39.12). Once he had crossed the Pyrenees he had only 50,000 infantry and 9,000 cavalry – rather more than half his original total but a much more manageable and unified fighting force.

From this point on we can only speculate as to the route that Hannibal took. It is not much help to be told by Polybius that he 'personally inspected the region and made a journey through the Alps for the purpose of learning and seeing' (3.48.12), as we cannot be certain that he followed Hannibal's exact path, even though he claimed to have 'questioned those who were present at these events.' How did he determine whether the men he questioned had actually been present or, if they had been present, whether they remembered the path they had taken? After crossing the Pyrenees, he made rapid progress, probably along the coast, facing little opposition from the local tribes. Towards the end of September he turned inland to cross the River Rhône further upstream. He deliberately skirted Massilia (modern Marseilles), a Greek colony at the mouth of the Rhône that was friendly to Rome, in part because he wanted to avoid a major encounter with the Romans until he arrived in Italy (Livy 21.31.3).

We do not know exactly where the crossing occurred. Polybius merely tells us it was about four days' march from the sea (3.42.1). A possible site is the modern town of Beaucaire, Roman 'Urgenum', which was destined to become an important stop along a later-constructed Roman road, the *via Domitia*, that would connect Italy to Spain. Finding that he was opposed on the left (or eastern) bank by a Gallic tribe known as the Volcae, Hannibal sent his second-in-command, Hanno, son of Bomilcar – not the same Hanno as the one whom he had left behind in northern Spain but his nephew – north up the right bank a distance of about 20 miles to a place where an island divided the Rhône in two. After making the crossing, Hanno followed the river downstream and caught the Volcae in the rear, thereby causing them to take flight.

Hannibal faced a formidable task in transporting his elephants across the river. Polybius, who was fascinated by the technique he adopted, says that he constructed piers some 200 feet long and attached a raft to each pier, covering them with earth so that the elephants would think they were still on dry land. As each one stepped onto the raft, it was towed across the river. The average elephant weighs five tons so the rafts had to be built very solidly. Very few elephants were lost, though many jumped into the river in fright when halfway across. It took Hannibal five days to complete the exercise. While the crossing was taking place he parlayed with some Gauls, who promised not only to join his cause, but also to indicate a route that would take him to Italy 'rapidly and safely and without undergoing any privations' (Polybius 3.44.7) – a nice deception, if ever there was one.

By heading inland Hannibal managed to avoid contact with the two Roman legions that had recently landed at Massilia under the command of the consul, Publius Cornelius Scipio, although he did not know they were in the vicinity. It was only now that the Romans learnt that he had crossed the Pyrenees. Previously they had no inkling of the fact that he was leading a land army to Italy. This says much both about the poor state of their military intelligence in this epoch and about the degree to which Hannibal had successfully concealed his intentions.

A skirmish between the two scouting parties took place, after which Publius Scipio marched up the Rhône in hot pursuit of the Carthaginians. However, he turned back when he found out that the enemy had a three-day start on him. Instead he dispatched most of his troops to Spain under the command of his elder brother Gnaeus Scipio with orders to attack Hannibal's bases in that country. This far-sighted decision meant that Spain would become an important theatre of war – as critical to its outcome as the war in Italy – since the Romans were able to prevent the supplies he had counted on from reaching him until the final years of his campaign. Publius Scipio sailed back to Italy, intending to protect Cisalpine Gaul (Gaul this-side-of-the-Alps, i.e. southern Gaul). By now he would have received reports of the size of Hannibal's army and was greatly alarmed.

According to Livy Hannibal rallied his troops and addressed them with these stirring words, 'alternately chiding and encouraging them' (21.30):

> I marvel at the fact that terror has suddenly invaded hearts that up till now have never experienced fear. For so many years you have been victorious. You did not leave Spain until all the peoples and lands that lie between two distant seas were in your grasp .... You crossed the Ebro in wrath to wipe out the name of Rome and free the whole world. At that time the march did not seem long to any of you, even though it might extend from the setting to the rising sun. But now, when you see that you have already completed most of the journey,

now that you have surmounted the Pyrenees with their savage tribes,
now that you have crossed the turbulent Rhône, even though many
thousands of Gauls sought to bar your way, and now that the Alps are
within sight with Italy on the other side – do you halt, claiming
exhaustion, at the very gates of your enemy's house?

The speech is almost certainly a complete invention. Even so, Hannibal's powers of persuasion were never more forcefully applied than
now. The army slogged on for four days till it came to an unidentified
location that is simply called 'The Island' in our sources. Here
Hannibal tarried for a few days, helping settle a dispute between two
brothers who headed rival groups of the same Gallic tribe. By favour-
ing the elder, he was able to obtain supplies for his men, including
clothing and footwear. He then marched for ten more days along the
banks of the River Isère until he reached the foothills of the Alps. It
was now late autumn.

Polybius tells us that 'the ascent over the Alps' took fifteen days,
although we do not know whether he means the whole journey across
the Alps, which totalled about 135 miles, or just the latter part of the
journey over the highest pass (3.56.3). There are at least half a dozen
passes that Hannibal might have taken, including Mont Genèvre,
Mont Cenis, and the Col de Clapier, and the debate as to which
should be preferred continues unabated to this day. It will probably
continue for ever, unless either elephant bones or a datable
Carthaginian artifact comes to light.

In the foothills of the Alps Hannibal encountered a hostile tribe
known as the Allobroges, who partly controlled the area. Eager to rob
him of his pack animals, his horses and other valuables, they had
positioned themselves on the high ground overlooking the path he
had to take. Discovering that they abandoned their posts at night,
Hannibal sent a force of picked men to occupy the ground. He won
a decisive encounter against the Allobroges on the second day and was

Fig. 4. Hannibal and his army crossing the Alps, attributed to Jacopo Ripanda, 1508-9.

able to rest his men on the third. The enemy reappeared, however, after he had crossed the River Durance. His plight was so wretched that one of his lieutenants, Hannibal Monomachus, even recommended resorting to cannibalism, which he roundly rejected (Polybius 9.24.6-7). The critical encounter with the tribe took place on the seventh day. Hannibal scored a convincing victory and the Allobroges did not trouble him again.

Hannibal began his descent 'on the twelfth day'. It proved as difficult as the ascent, since a fresh fall of snow had formed over the ice, making it extremely treacherous underfoot. At one point a landslide had obliterated the road for several hundred yards and his Numidians had to build a new path. Livy, but not Polybius, tells the famous story of his engineers using vinegar (or sour wine) to break up previously heated rocks (21.37.2-3). The story is highly improbable because, as Livy himself indicates, the procedure would have required an immense amount of wood. Very likely it is simply a rhetorical invention, intended to add drama and dash to the narrative.

Fig. 5. 'Hannibal crossing the Alps.' Drawing by John
Leech from Gilbert Abbott à Beckett, *The Comic History
of Rome*, 1852.

Having reached the plains of the Po Valley 'on the fifteenth day'
in the tribal region of the Taurini (roughly the location of modern
Turin), Hannibal rested his men for three days. The crossing had
taken a very heavy toll on man and beast. His army had been reduced
to '12,000 African infantry, 8,000 Iberian infantry, and not more
than 6,000 cavalry' – less than half the size it had been after he had
crossed the Pyrenees (Polybius 3.56.4). Though the numbers prior to
crossing the Alps had doubtless been exaggerated, the proportion of

soldiers lost may well be substantially correct. Lucius Cincius Alimentus, who was captured by the Carthaginians, said that Hannibal admitted he had lost 36,000 men. He had no reason to exaggerate this figure. Most of his casualties were due to desertions and weather conditions, rather than to enemy action. In addition, many of his men were suffering from frostbite when they descended into Italy. Polybius states that they looked 'more like beasts than men in outer appearance and general condition' (3.60.6). Hannibal also lost a large proportion of his horses and pack animals. We do not know how many of his elephants survived the march but there is no report of any casualties.

Hannibal arrived in Italy some time between mid-October and late November. It had taken him five to six months to cover the 940 miles from Carthago Nova to the valley of the River Po. Though it is impossible to calculate accurately, he had averaged something like five to six miles per day.

6

The Invasion of Italy

It is pretty staggering to contemplate that Hannibal challenged the might of Rome with an army of only 26,000, but there is no reason to doubt the figures that he inscribed in the temple of Juno Lacinia. Once the news that he had successfully scaled the Alps reached Rome, consternation gripped its people. They were unprepared for a war on home territory and overwhelmed by the speed of his progress. Publius Cornelius Scipio, having returned to Italy, awaited Hannibal on the plains of the River Po. He was eager to be the first Roman general to face him in battle. The Senate ordered Scipio's fellow-consul, Tiberius Sempronius Longus, whose fleet was moored at Lilybaeum (modern Marsala) at the western tip of Sicily preparatory to its departure for Africa, to return to Italy without delay. The Romans had been planning to launch an invasion, knowing there was no Carthaginian general of any note in the region. But Hannibal had pre-empted them and Africa was now safe.

Some time in late autumn Scipio crossed to the north bank of the River Po to oppose Hannibal's advance. Hannibal marched eastwards along the same bank, and the two met at the River Ticinus (modern Ticino), near the modern town of Pavia in southwest Lombardy, in late November or early December. Polybius reports that before the encounter took place Hannibal asked a pair of Allobrogian prisoners whom he had captured when crossing the Alps whether they would be willing to fight each other to the death, promising that the victor would be free to return home (3.62.6-63.14). They agreed and a fight

THE ITALIAN PENINSULA

took place, after which the victor rode off free. Hannibal supposedly used the incident to demonstrate to his men that they faced a similar choice between conquering and dying. Livy tells the same story but claims that several pairs of combatants fought, not just one pair (21.42).

In the ensuing cavalry encounter at the River Ticinus, Hannibal got the better of the Romans. Scipio himself suffered a serious wound and according to the family tradition was saved by his seventeen-year-old son and namesake, the future victor at Zama. Though the number of Roman casualties was probably quite low, the defeat had a debilitating effect on Roman morale. Thousands of Gauls now

71

Fig. 6. 'Hannibal disguising himself.' Drawing by John Leech from Gilbert Abbott à Beckett, *The Comic History of Rome*, 1852.

joined Hannibal's ranks, though he was apparently mistrustful of their allegiance. Polybius tells us that in the winter of 217, fearing that one of them might make an attempt upon his life, Hannibal took to wearing a variety of wigs to avoid detection. He describes it disparagingly as a 'typically Phoenician stunt' (3.78.1-4). The ruse reminds us of Saddam Hussein's use of look-alikes in the Iraq War.

Scipio withdrew to his base at Placentia (modern Piacenza). His confidence had been badly shaken. Some time in December he marched towards the River Trebbia, a tributary of the Po, where he awaited Sempronius' arrival. The journey from Lilybaeum to Ariminum (modern Rimini) took Sempronius forty days (Polybius 3.68.14). When he arrived in Scipio's camp, Scipio handed over the command of the army to him and urged him to postpone engaging Hannibal in battle, his argument being that the Gauls would desert to the Romans if he remained inactive (3.70.1-8). Hannibal had repeatedly told the Gauls living between the Trebbia and the Po 'that he had come at their request, to liberate them' but to little effect (Livy 21.52.4). In frustration he had sent a detachment to ravage their land as far as the River Po. As a result they had appealed to the Romans, and though Scipio doubted their loyalty as allies, he still saw it as advantageous to draw them away from Hannibal.

Scipio failed to dissuade his headstrong colleague from offering battle, however, and the two armies engaged around the time of the winter solstice (21 December). Being a client of the Scipionic family (see above, p. 33), Polybius was naturally eager to present Scipio in the most favourable light. His suggestion, later adopted by Livy, that Sempronius was solely responsible for the ill-fated decision to join battle is therefore suspect.

The two armies were roughly equal in size with 40,000 men apiece, though Hannibal's cavalry greatly outnumbered its Roman counterpart. At dawn Hannibal sent his infantry across the river to harass Sempronius' camp, hoping to provoke the Romans into an engagement. The tactic worked and Sempronius led his army across the left bank in a northerly direction till he arrived in open, flat terrain. There he drew up his army with the river behind him. It was raining heavily and by the time he had deployed his men they were hungry and chilled to the bone. By contrast the Carthaginians were well-fed and rested, having had nothing to do except await Sempronius' arrival.

Hannibal's cavalry easily routed the Roman cavalry. It then attacked the Roman infantry on the wings, while a contingent of 2,000 crack troops under the command of his younger brother Mago, which had previously been hidden from view, attacked the infantry from the rear. The battle was hard fought; the Roman wings eventually gave way, though the centre broke through the opposing Gauls and Libyans. About three-quarters of the Roman army was destroyed, probably about 30,000 men in total. Polybius says that Hannibal lost very few Spanish and Libyan troops and that most of those who fell were Gauls (3.74.10).

Sempronius later claimed that he would have vanquished the Carthaginians but for the bad weather – a claim that Polybius rejected, not unnaturally given his allegiance to Scipio (3.75.1-3). Hannibal had chosen both the time and the terrain, and had added an element of surprise. These were to be the hallmarks of his Italian campaign. Trebbia was a foretaste of things to come. It was also the only battle in Italy in which Hannibal was able to use his elephants, as all but one died soon after. Incidentally, this is the last time that we hear of any *sunedroi*, representatives of the Carthaginian Senate, who acted in an advisory capacity (Polybius 3.71.5; see above, p. 20). From now on Hannibal was his own boss.

Livy tells us that the Romans were devastated by news of the defeat and hourly expected to see Hannibal outside the city walls, though this may be later propaganda intended to underscore the parlousness of their situation. Hannibal attacked a magazine near Placentia but was wounded and had to withdraw. Later he successfully besieged a magazine at Victumulae, the exact site of which has not been identified. This (not Trebbia) was his first victory on the Italian peninsula. Livy claims that after the inhabitants had surrendered, Hannibal gave the order to sack the town, thereby unleashing 'every kind of lust and cruelty and inhuman insolence' (*omne* [sc. *genus*] *libidinis crudelitatisque et inhumanae superbiae*; 21.57.13-14).

The winter was particularly severe and many of Hannibal's men died. His horses contracted mange and all but one of his elephants perished. All the effort of getting the animals across the Alps had come to nothing in the end, though it had enhanced the legendary quality of his march and sowed terror in the hearts of many Romans.

6. The Invasion of Italy

After releasing his non-Roman prisoners in the hope that his generosity would motivate Rome's allies to revolt, Hannibal broke camp in the early spring and marched in the direction of Etruria. Riding through the deep marshes of the River Arno on the back of his sole surviving elephant – probably the one with a broken tusk called Surus or 'The Syrian' – he contracted ophthalmia, an inflammation of the eye. He refused to stop and receive treatment, and lost at least the partial sight of one eye (Polybius 3.79.12; Pliny, *Natural History* 8.5.11).

The consuls for 217 were Caius Flaminius Nepos and Gnaeus Servilius Geminus. To block Hannibal's advance into Etruria, Flaminius marched to Arretium (modern Arezzo, the most northeasterly of the Etruscan cities), while Geminus advanced as far as Ariminum to bar his path along the Adriatic coast. Hannibal managed to swing past Flaminius' army, however, and began burning the countryside with the intention of provoking him into action. Polybius presents Flaminius as rash and imprudent (3.80.1-81.12), whereas Livy suggests he was merely high-spirited (22.1-10). Either way, Hannibal had taken his measure, as previously he had taken the measure of Sempronius.

On the morning of 21 June, the day of the summer solstice, Flaminius woke up to discover that Hannibal had raised camp and given him the slip. Fearing that he was advancing on Rome, he set off in hot pursuit with his army of 25,000 men, without having sent out any scouts to reconnoitre in advance. Hannibal had laid an ambush at the northeast corner of Lake Trasimene, concealing his troops in the hills above (see map overleaf). It was, in Livy's phrase, 'a place born for an ambush' (22.4.2), and one has to wonder how Flaminius can have been so stupid, notwithstanding his desperate anxiety to catch up with Hannibal, who was at this point only 85 miles from Rome. The Carthaginians maintained perfect discipline until Flaminius' entire column had advanced into the narrow passage

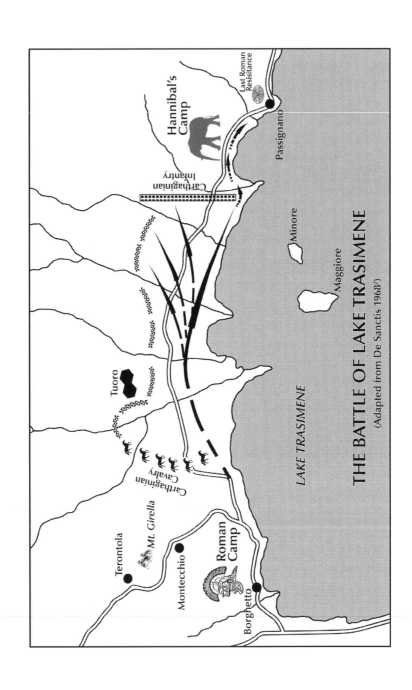

THE BATTLE OF LAKE TRASIMENE
(Adapted from De Sanctis 1968²)

between the hills and the shoreline. Hannibal then gave the order to attack. A mist was rising off the lake and the Romans could hardly see the enemy as they fell on them from above. Caught off guard, they were massacred. Polybius paints the horrifying picture of Roman infantrymen standing in the water up to their necks, vainly imploring the Carthaginian cavalry to spare them (3.84.9-10).

The battle lasted three hours. Fabius Pictor, who is the source for both Polybius (3.84.7) and Livy (22.7.2), reported that 15,000 Romans perished. Among them was Flaminius, slain by a Gaul. We are told that Hannibal wanted to bury him with full military honours but was unable to identify his body. The pitiful remnant of his army made its way back to Rome. This was not the only disaster that the Romans suffered around this time. Flaminius' consular colleague Servilius Geminus, who had set out from Ariminum to join him, had sent a detachment of 4,000 cavalry under Caius Centenius in advance. A few days after the battle the cavalry was intercepted by Hannibal's lieutenant Maharbal. Many men were either killed or captured.

Rome's defeat sent shock waves through the Greek-speaking world. Polybius puts a speech into the mouth of an Aetolian called Agelaus to the effect that it was obvious to all with even a basic understanding of international politics that the outcome of the war would have profound consequences for the Mediterranean world (5.104.3; see below, p. 130). When the news of the catastrophe reached Rome, the urban praetor Marcus Pomponius abruptly announced to the populace, 'We have been defeated in a great battle.' Distraught wives, mothers and fathers waited at the city gates in the hope of identifying their relatives among the survivors (Livy 22.7.6-14). The Senate remained in session from dawn to sunset for several days – seemingly an unprecedented occurrence. Shortly afterwards, to add to their woes, the people received news of Centenius' defeat.

Hannibal marched eastwards through Umbria to the Adriatic

coast, his troops so burdened with booty that they staggered under its weight (Polybius 3.86.9-10). He continued on his destructive path as far south as Arpi in Apulia, killing every able-bodied Italian he met, whether Roman or not. To deal with the crisis Quintus Fabius Maximus was appointed dictator. Fabius was a seasoned warrior and an experienced politician. Now in his late fifties, he had twice been consul and had held the position of censor, with power to scrutinise the membership of the Senate. He had been among the delegation to Carthage that had demanded the surrender of Hannibal before the outbreak of war. The power or *imperium* of a dictator, who at this time was appointed solely to deal with military crises, was well-nigh absolute. All serving magistrates were subordinate to him. His term of office was limited to six months. He was assisted by a *magister equitum* or master of cavalry. Customarily a dictator was appointed by a consul or other magistrate with *imperium* on the authorisation of the Senate, whereas the *magister equitum* was appointed by the dictator himself. On this occasion, however, since the sole surviving consul Servilius Geminus was in the field and could not travel to Rome, the Senate appointed both magistrates. Fabius' *magister equitum* was a former consul called Marcus Minucius Rufus, a man many years his junior.

Fearing that Hannibal intended to attack Rome, Fabius made it his immediate task to repair the city walls and break down the bridges over the Tiber. The help of the gods was earnestly solicited. The Sibylline books, collections of oracular utterances written in Greek and ascribed to a sibyl or prophetess, were consulted. A second sacrifice was performed to the war god Mars, duplicating the one that had inaugurated the campaigning season of 217. In addition, the gods were invited to a *lectisternium*; that is to say, their images were placed on couches and offered a banquet. Though the ritual had first been performed in 399, this was the first occasion that the twelve principal gods of the Roman pantheon had been fused with their

Greek counterparts, Jupiter being equated with Zeus, Juno with Hera, and so on. The Romans also vowed a temple to Venus Erycina or Venus of Mount Eryx (Monte San Giuliano in northwestern Sicily) on the Capitoline Hill, the most prestigious religious site in Rome. Eryx had been the last stronghold of Hamilcar during the First Punic War and this was an appeal to its tutelary deity to side with the Romans in the present war. Venus Erycina thus became the first foreign deity to be worshipped inside the *pomerium* or sacred boundary surrounding the city of Rome. The fact that the Senate sought to alleviate the crisis by resorting to so many religious expedients is a measure of the panic that Hannibal had instilled in the Roman people.

In the event Hannibal did not attack Rome. Instead, as we've seen, he turned eastwards, hoping to encourage Rome's allies to defect. Dexter Hoyos (*Hannibal* [Exeter 2008] 51) calls this 'perhaps his most important decision in the war' – even more important than his decision not to attack Rome after Cannae. Meanwhile Fabius raised two new legions, which, if Hannibal had remained in the region, he would not have been able to do. If ever Hannibal wasted an opportunity, this was it.

Fabius' strategy was to avoid pitched battle at all costs and employ guerilla tactics to harass Hannibal's column and foraging parties, with the intention of eventually wearing him down. It proved bitterly divisive, since it left Hannibal free to ravage the Italian countryside while the Roman army looked on helplessly. The dictator gambled on Rome's allies remaining loyal, but in view of the fact that he issued an order that those within reach of Hannibal's army should adopt a scorched earth policy by burning their homes and crops and withdrawing within their walls, it was not without considerable risk. It also made Rome dependent on imported corn, primarily from Sicily and Sardinia. It is a tribute both to Fabius' determination and to the extraordinary discipline of the Romans that he was able to implement it even for a short period of time. It also pointed up the limitations of Hannibal's own strategy. Lacking a permanent base in Italy from which to conduct operations, he and his men were an army on the march, at perpetual risk of being worn down by attrition.

Fabius left Rome at the head of an army of four legions plus an equal number of allies (i.e. about 40,000 men in total) in August. He marched eastwards through the mountains of Samnium into Apulia in pursuit of his quarry. At a town called Aecae Hannibal offered him battle, but Fabius refused to be drawn. Hannibal then left Apulia and doubled back westwards through Samnium, along the route that Fabius had just taken, into the plain in Campania known as the *ager Falernus*. Campania was important to him because it was very fertile and possessed several important ports, notably Cumae and Neapolis (Naples); see map opposite. He was eager to secure a port so that he could establish a regular line of communication with Carthage. Having pitched camp near Casilinum, he proceeded to ravage the countryside with his cavalry, while Fabius looked on from the mountains. With his customary guile Hannibal gave orders to his men not to ravage Fabius' estate in the area – the same tactic incidentally which the Spartans had employed in the Peloponnesian War to undermine Pericles' authority by suggesting that they were in cahoots together – and in an exchange of prisoners he handed over 247 more men than he received back. Both actions were intended to cast doubts on Fabius' loyalty.

As the year drew to a close Hannibal headed back eastwards again, where he intended to set up his winter quarters. It is unclear why he chose to abandon Campania at this point, particularly since it offered him easier communication with Carthage. It was a decision that very nearly cost him dear, since Fabius succeeded in penning him in on both sides of a pass. To escape Hannibal carried out one of his most daring ruses. He tied blazing faggots to the horns of a herd of oxen and drove them up onto a mountain. The Romans, suspecting they

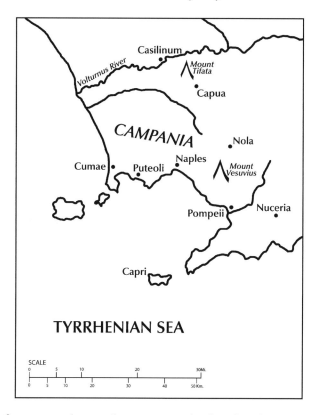

were facing a night attack, were completely taken by surprise and Hannibal broke through their lines to safety. Fabius had been outwitted and humiliated, and his lack of enterprise was deeply resented by his compatriots. He was dubbed 'Hannibal's *paedagogus*' – *paedagogus* was the name for a slave, often elderly, who accompanied his young master to school – and shortly afterwards he was recalled to Rome. Minucius Felix, his *magister equitum*, who had scored a notable success against Hannibal, was given powers equal to those of the dictator, and each of them was assigned two legions apiece.

Not long afterwards Hannibal enticed Minucius into an engagement at Mons Calenus, near Larinum (modern Larino). If Fabius had

81

not come to his rescue, Minucius' army would have been destroyed. Acknowledging his error, Minucius resigned as dictator and resumed the subordinate position of *magister equitum*. Meanwhile Hannibal established his winter quarters in Apulia. In Spain, however, the war was going decidedly Rome's way. Gnaeus Scipio drew Hannibal's brother Hasdrubal into a naval battle at the mouth of the Ebro. Hasdrubal's losses were heavy and 25 ships were captured, though he himself escaped. The Spanish campaign would have profound consequences for the outcome of the war.

7

The Battle of Cannae

Fabius Maximus' dictatorship lapsed in December and Caius Terentius Varro and Lucius Aemilius Paullus were elected consuls for the year 216. It was a peaceful transition and it is doubtful whether Fabius himself had been expecting his strategy to be implemented for a longer period of time. It had merely been a stopgap measure. In either late 217 or early 216 the Senate began doubling the strength of Rome's army – from four to eight legions. Since each legion comprised some 4,500 to 5,000 men, the total size of the Roman army would have been approximately 80,000, if we include, as we probably should, an equal number of allies. This meant that half the Roman troops (and no doubt at least an equal proportion of allied troops) who faced Hannibal in 216 were untested in battle and probably capable of only limited military manoeuvres.

No military action is recorded for the first half of the year. Hannibal's spies would have informed him that the Romans were greatly increasing the size of their army and this gave him plenty of time to plan his strategy. He moved out of his winter quarters at Gerunium in Apulia probably some time in June and headed south to a hilltop town called Cannae (modern Canne), situated about 70 miles to the south. Cannae was of considerable military significance, since it controlled access to the Apennines and thus to the route to the grain fields in the south of Italy. It was also an important supply base for the Romans in southern Italy. The town was located on the south bank of the River Aufidius (modern Ofanto), the only river that

runs through the Apennines. Hannibal chose the location as a battlefield because it was situated in open, flat country and provided an
excellent opportunity for his cavalry to perform to best advantage.

Varro and Paullus joined forces, perhaps at Gerunium, towards
the end of July, and from there followed Hannibal's route south to
Cannae. Their infantry is thought to have outnumbered Hannibal's
infantry by 2:1 (by 80,000 to 40,000), proof that the Romans were
relying on the weight of their legions to crush the enemy. Many in
the Carthaginian ranks were amazed by the size of the opposing army,
the largest that the Romans had ever put in the field. It was on this
occasion that Hannibal joked with an officer called Gisgo that 'what
was more amazing still was that none of the men facing them was
called Gisgo' (above p. 24). His observation was greeted with laughter
and a tense situation expertly defused.

When two Roman consuls served in the same army, they held
command on alternate days. This lent itself to obvious exploitation
by Hannibal, who again apprised himself of the very different tem-
peraments of the two consuls. According to Polybius, Varro was
much more eager to engage the enemy than Paullus, though we
should note that Paullus was the (biological as opposed to adoptive)
grandfather of Polybius' patron, so his testimony, yet again, should
be treated with caution. Even so, it is entirely believable that Varro
was more aggressive and that Hannibal managed to lure the Romans
into battle on a day when Varro was in command for this reason. As
the tactics employed by Fabius Maximus had demonstrated, this was
an era in which, barring an ambush, it was virtually impossible to
force a general to engage against his will, and the day before the battle
took place Paullus had declined Hannibal's offer.

On 2 August Varro led his army out of camp with the intention
of offering battle. He probably drew his army up on the right (or
southwest bank) of the Aufidius, though scholars continue to debate
this issue (see plan on p. 86). The river provided protection to his

battle line on the right. Varro placed his Roman and allied infantry in the centre, his Roman cavalry on the right wing, and his allied cavalry on the left. The depth of his centre was between 50 and 70 ranks. His entire battle line was probably over a mile in length. His intention was to attack the enemy head-on by presenting an impenetrable wall. It was a simple but time-tested strategy, which the lack of manoeuvrability of his infantry demanded of him.

Hannibal extended his line as far as the Romans to give the appearance of equality, though it was nothing like as deep. The front ranks consisted of his Iberian and Gallic troops. To boost morale he took up position in or close to the front rank alongside his brother Mago. He kept his superior, Libyan infantry in the rear. Shortly before the battle commenced, he ordered his infantry to advance and create an outward-bulging arc. It was his expectation and intention that the arc would cave inwards under pressure, though without actually giving way. It was a high-risk strategy, characteristic of Hannibal, because if it collapsed the Romans would sweep forward en masse and the battle would be lost. He placed his cavalry on the wings, Spanish and Gallic on the left, Numidian on the right. It greatly outnumbered the Roman cavalry – by about 10,000 to 6,000 – and was much superior in training and expertise. It was the cavalry that determined the outcome of the battle.

Though many details of the battle are unclear, Hannibal's strategy was to entice the Romans forward into the centre of his infantry line and then encircle them, which is exactly what happened. As the Roman infantry thrust its way forward into the now inward-bulging arc that opened up invitingly before it, the Libyan infantry closed in on it from both sides. Meanwhile the cavalry on the flanks, having easily defeated its opponents, swung round to attack the Roman infantry in the rear.

What followed was a bloodbath. John Lazenby (*Oxford Classical Dictionary*, 3rd edn [Oxford 2003] 286) comments, 'The Roman

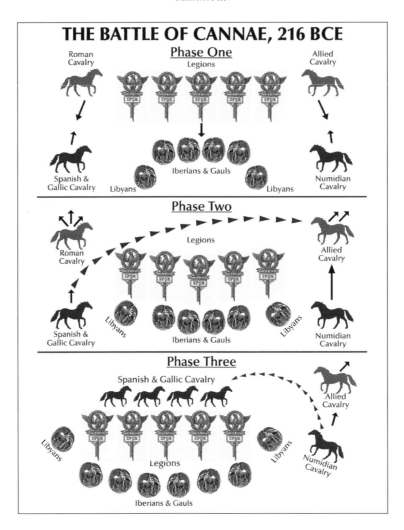

army perhaps suffered higher casualties in a single day's fighting than any other western army before or since.' That means heavier casualties than at Gettysburg or on the first day of the Somme. In fact it was the worst defeat the Roman army ever sustained. Polybius puts the dead at 70,000 (3.117.4); Livy, more credibly, at 50,000, including

4,500 cavalry (22.59.5; 60.14). Both the consul Aemilius Paullus and the former master of horses Minucius Rufus were among the fallen, together with approximately 80 men of senatorial rank, many others of equestrian rank, and 29 of the 48 military tribunes. Perhaps as many as 10,000 were taken prisoner. Some of the injured Romans buried their heads in the soil in a pathetic effort to choke themselves to death – a horrific picture. Hannibal gave honourable burial to Paullus, but the rest of the enemy dead were left on the field to rot. He perhaps lacked the resources to bury such a large number and, besides, the Romans had fled the field. Soon afterwards the Romans suffered yet another disaster: the consul-elect Lucius Postumus was ambushed and killed by the Gauls in the north of Italy.

Hannibal's losses amounted to 6,000, of whom 4,000 were Gauls. Appian, writing three and a half centuries later, claims that when Hannibal saw the bravest of his friends among the dead he burst into tears and said that he did not want another such victory (*Hannibalic War* 7.26). The general who experiences existential Angst in the aftermath of a historic victory was a literary topos and the story is almost certainly apocryphal. Even so, it is not improbable that Hannibal's elation was tempered by a sober sense of reality. Though in absolute terms he had won a devastating victory, he could ill afford the estimated loss of 2,000 of his crack troops.

Only about 14,500 Romans escaped either death or captivity, among them Varro, who fled to Venusia, some 50 miles to the west, with about 50 or 70 cavalrymen. A larger group of survivors took refuge in Canusium, about 25 miles to the west. Livy tells us that the younger Scipio, having been elected commander by popular vote, proceeded to rally his men with the following rousing oath: 'I swear never to desert the Roman Republic nor allow any Roman soldier to do so either. If I knowingly break my word, may Jupiter Optimus Maximus (Greatest and Best) destroy me, my house, my family, and my possessions' (22.53.10-11). Livy's point is that the man who was destined to become Hannibal's nemesis burned with a motivational intensity that equalled Hannibal's – and with an equal degree of patriotic fervour. Livy is also at pains to emphasise that the townsfolk in Venusia and Canusium competed with each other to demonstrate their goodwill to the Romans in their hour of need. Eventually Varro joined forces with Scipio at Canusium.

The day after the battle Hannibal ordered his men to strip all the gold rings from the corpses of Roman senators and knights. He later dispatched the rings to the Carthaginian Senate in the safekeeping of his brother Mago with a request for reinforcements. It is now, according to tradition, that his cavalry commander Maharbal told him that, if he marched on Rome, he would dine on the Capitol in five days (Livy 22.51.2). Logistically speaking the suggestion was preposterous. Rome lies about 300 miles from Cannae. It would have taken Hannibal at least fifteen days to complete the march, especially as it lay through mountainous terrain. When Hannibal declined to accept his advice, Maharbal observed, 'You know how to win a battle but you do not know how to make use of it.' Livy declares at this point in his narrative, 'This delay is generally thought to have been the salvation of Rome and of her empire.' Polybius does not report this anecdote and it may have been invented as a way of highlighting how close Rome came to annihilation. The question why Hannibal failed to launch an attack on Rome in the weeks, if not days after Cannae has none the less exercised military as well as scholarly minds ever since. The simplest and most plausible explanation is that he lacked the forces to conduct a protracted siege and never envisaged the capture of the city as a way to win the war. As we noted in the previous chapter, he could, moreover, have attacked Rome after the Battle of Lake Trasimene.

Livy claims that Hannibal told his Roman prisoners that it was not his intention to exterminate their race but simply to restore his nation's *dignitas* (self-respect) and establish its *imperium* (domina-

Fig. 7. Marble statue of Hannibal counting the rings of the Roman knights killed at the Battle of Cannae, by Sébastien Slodtz, 1704.

tion). Though *dignitas* and *imperium* are quintessentially Roman values, Hannibal may well have said something to this effect (22.58.3). However, the speeches of enemy commanders as reported by Roman historians are likely to be pure invention, and this one is no exception. So for the most part are the reported speeches of Roman commanders. Only two 'transcripts' have survived from the entirety of Roman history – the speech that the Emperor Claudius delivered on the admission of Gauls to the Senate in AD 46 and the speech that the Emperor Hadrian delivered on a ceremonial occasion while touring the province of Africa in AD 128.

The initial report that reached Rome was that there were no survivors. On the recommendation of Fabius Maximus, the Senate prohibited weeping and forbade any citizen to leave Rome. Once again the Romans invoked their gods. Earlier in the year two Vestal Virgins, the religious officials charged with the task of safeguarding the sacred hearth, had been convicted of breaking their vow of chastity. One had been buried alive; the other had committed suicide. A man who had been accused of corrupting them was now scourged to death. The Sibylline books were again consulted and this time Quintus Fabius Pictor was dispatched to Delphi to seek the advice of Apollo. The Romans also revived the barbaric practice of live burial in the case of a Gallic man and woman and a Greek man and woman, who were interred in the Forum Boarium (or Cattle Market) in the centre of Rome. The victims were stand-ins, so to speak, for the Gauls who had sacked Rome in the early fourth century BC and for the Greeks who had conquered the Trojans – Rome's supposed ancestors – centuries earlier. They were, in other words, archetypal scapegoats. Though Livy claims that live burial was 'alien to Roman religion' (22.57.6), a previous instance is recorded for 225, when the Romans were anticipating the Gallic invasion that took place later that year (Plutarch, *Marcellus* 3.4). The action is a clear indicator of the desperation that gripped the people.

7. The Battle of Cannae

As everyone knows, Hannibal did not march on Rome. Instead he rested his army and sent a delegation to Rome under the leadership of a cavalry officer called Carthalo, offering to ransom his Roman prisoners and negotiate peace terms. To increase the stakes, he sent ten, presumably highly distinguished prisoners along with the delegation (Livy 22.58.6). When the Senate got wind of Carthalo's arrival, it ordered him out of Roman territory immediately. It did, however, allow entry to the Roman prisoners who accompanied him. After what was no doubt an extremely emotional debate, it courageously decided not to ransom a single one of them and sent them back to Hannibal.

Varro now returned to Rome to make his report to the Senate, as custom required. Livy tells us that a large crowd went to meet him and congratulate him 'for not having despaired of the Republic' (22.61.14); that is to say, for having had the courage to face the music rather than go into voluntary exile. Had he been a Carthaginian general, as Livy notes, he would have been punished to the extremity of the law. It is at this point that Polybius provides an excursus on the character of the Roman Republican constitution, which, from his viewpoint, gives the best explanation for Rome's resilience and strength, though we might note that he either misunderstood, or was misinformed about, certain important features of that constitution, including the role of the Senate.

The Senate immediately began raising a new army of four legions by enlisting those as young as seventeen. It may have lowered the property qualification for military service at this time. It also enlisted 6,000 debtors and 8,000 slaves. The survivors of Cannae were formed into two legions and sent to Sicily, where they served throughout the war, both as a punishment and as a warning. Marcus Junius Pera was appointed dictator with Tiberius Sempronius Gracchus as *magister equitum*. Marcus Claudius Marcellus was put in command of the forces at Canusium.

When Carthalo returned with the news that the Romans were not prepared to negotiate, Hannibal executed a number of his prisoners, presumably the most eminent. It is unclear whether this violent act was a spontaneous outburst of anger or whether he hoped to sway the Senate even at the eleventh hour. He sold the rest into slavery. We can only imagine what impact the Roman refusal to sue for peace had upon him – first scorn, next bewilderment, then some measure of admiration, and finally, I suspect, frustration, even perhaps despondency. His finest hour was already fast receding, notwithstanding the fact that his victory had made Carthage, for a few brief years, the most powerful state in the Mediterranean.

8

The Wilderness Years

Though the Second Punic War can be justly termed the Hannibalic War, from 216 onwards other regions besides Italy became increasingly drawn within its orbit, including Sardinia, Sicily, mainland Greece and Spain, where Hannibal never set foot during the war. As a result his story no longer held centre stage in the larger scheme of things, as the Italian campaign became only one among a number of factors that contributed to the final outcome of the war. Despite this fact, Hannibal remained nominally in charge of Carthage's war effort, though he seems increasingly to have lost control over events in Spain.

Although I have entitled this chapter 'The Wilderness Years', Hannibal's trajectory was not all downhill from 216 onwards. As Lazenby (*Hannibal's War* [Warminster1978] vi) has pointed out, 209, rather than 216, might justly be considered the moment of his greatest success, since this was when twelve Latin colonies refused to contribute men to the Roman army and when the Latin League came closest to disintegration. Even so, it is difficult to resist the conclusion that from 216 onwards his resolve and belief in his mission were increasingly put to the test. For 216 to 202 we are primarily dependent on Livy, as we lack Polybius' narrative for the fourteen years from Cannae to the final showdown at Zama.

Hannibal's failure to move on Rome in the weeks after Cannae cannot be lightly dismissed. It was the last chance he would have to bring the city to its knees, and even if he had not succeeded, by merely blockading it he would have humbled it in the eyes of its allies and hindered the Romans from building up a new army. His own was seriously reduced in numbers. One estimate puts his total fighting strength at 42,800. Recruiting from the Gauls and the Italians was no longer an adequate solution. He needed crack troops from home. Accordingly, as we have seen, he sent his brother Mago to Carthage to request reinforcements. In the presence of the Senate Mago ordered his attendants to heap the gold rings that had been removed from the fingers of Roman senators and knights as proof of the scale of his brother's victory. This, we should note in passing, was an age in which hard data was impossible to come by. According to Livy, the quantity of rings amounted to either three and a half pecks or, more probably in his view, one peck. Even if the lower figure is true, this is still impressive testimony to the fact that so many men of senatorial rank had been prepared to give their lives in defence of the Republic – a markedly different state of affairs to the one that exists in western warfare today (23.12.1). Though Mago's request for reinforcements met with opposition, the Senate eventually agreed to dispatch 4,000 Numidians and 40 elephants to Italy. It also authorised the sending of a large force from Spain.

Hannibal devoted the rest of the campaigning season to undermining Rome's control over her allies, which he achieved with some success. He first marched into Samnium, where a number of towns defected to him, and then to the fertile southern region of Campania. He also sent a detachment initially under the command of his brother Mago, then, when Mago left for Carthage, under his nephew Hanno, to the south of Italy, where a number of towns joined his cause. However, it is unclear whether these defections added much to his military strength in the long run, as he was not in a position to impose regular conscription for fear of alienating his new-found allies.

In hopes of securing a port to receive the reinforcements from Africa, he initially turned his sights on Neapolis (modern Naples), the most important Greek city in the region, but was deterred from laying siege to it by the size and strength of its walls (see map on p. 81). Instead he made a treaty with the inhabitants of Capua (modern Santa Maria di Capua Vetere), promising them 'that their town would become the capital of all Italy and that from it the Romans along with all other nations should derive their laws' (Livy 23.10.2). The Capuans, who had been subordinate to the Romans, had a hankering for role reversal. Hannibal's offer gives us some inkling of what his ultimate aim may have been – to downgrade, rather than destroy Rome. The Romans were naturally outraged by the presumptuousness of their former allies and later wreaked terrible vengeance on them.

After making a failed attempt upon Nola, which lay eighteen miles east of Naples, Hannibal returned to Capua, where he wintered. Appian claims that he now abandoned himself to 'unaccustomed luxury and love-making' (*Hannibalic War* 43). This is the only evidence we have that he ever strayed from his military objective or that he had wild, promiscuous sex. Likewise Livy reports that his men gave themselves over to 'sleep, wine, feasts, prostitutes, baths and idleness' (23.18.12), the effects of which, assuming the claim is true, would have been all the more deleterious owing to their unfamiliarity with such pleasures. Consequently, when Hannibal led them out of Capua the following spring, 'no trace of their former discipline remained'. Polybius, however, fails to corroborate these charges. Quite possibly they are based on the assumption that Hannibal and his men were sorely in need of a break from their punishing routine. As the campaigning season came to an end, Hannibal could well take pride in his achievement. It had indeed been an *annus mirabilis* of sorts, though he had crucially failed to take a port.

In 215 the Carthaginian Senate mounted its greatest effort on Hannibal's behalf. Bomilcar (possibly a brother-in-law of the Barcids) landed at Locri Epizephyrii (modern Locri, formerly called Gerace) in Calabria with the reinforcements that the Senate had promised to Mago. Himilco, a member of the Barcid clan, arrived in Sicily with a force of 28,000 men and twelve elephants. He, along with many of his men, died of the plague, however, and the enterprise was a failure. It was also a year that saw Rome's fortunes rise substantially. Hannibal's brother Hasdrubal, who had been ordered by the Senate to march into Italy, suffered another defeat on the Ebro River at a small town called Ibera. In consequence, a force of 12,000 foot and 1,500 horse that had been earmarked for Italy under the command of his other brother Mago was now diverted to Spain to relieve him and several Spanish towns defected to Rome. It would be the better part of a decade before Hasdrubal could bring his brother the reinforcements he so desperately needed. In the interim Hannibal became more and more dependent upon Gallic and Italian manpower. Had his brother reached Italy in 215, there's no telling what impact this would have had upon the war, particularly as Philip V of Macedon now allied himself to the Carthaginian cause (see below). So by saving Spain, the Scipios had immeasurably assisted the situation in Italy.

Hannibal established his base at Mount Tifata, overlooking Capua, though he failed to take either Cumae (modern Cuma) or Nola. Livy explains that his army had become enfeebled by 'Campanian-style luxury, wine-bibbing, whoring and all manner of dissipation', the consequence being that 'Capua was Hannibal's Cannae' (23.45.2-4). It was essentially the same verdict that he had delivered on Hannibal the previous year and it again reflects Livy's characteristic emphasis upon discipline. Morale was so low in the Carthaginian ranks that 1,200 Numidian and Spanish horse defected to the Romans. Hannibal spent the winter at Arpi (a town about five miles north of modern Foggia) in Apulia.

On the positive side, the fifteen-year-old Hieronymus, tyrant of Syracuse, entered into negotiations with Hannibal. Though Syracuse was nominally independent, in practice it took orders from Rome and had been a loyal ally under its previous ruler, Hieronymus' grandfather Hiero. At the prompting of his advisors, however, Hieronymus now sought to make Syracuse dominant throughout Sicily and saw an alliance with Carthage as the best way to achieve this end. Learning of his intention, the Romans immediately dispatched a joint military and naval force under Marcellus to lay siege to the port city. Its people held out for two years, greatly assisted by the resourcefulness of Archimedes (see below, p. 99).

The war now began to extend into the eastern Mediterranean. Philip V of Macedon concluded a treaty with Hannibal in 215, thereby initiating the so-called First Macedonian War. The terms of the treaty make clear that Hannibal expected Rome to survive the war – further proof that his intention was to cripple rather than destroy it (Polybius 7.9). Philip was seeking control over the eastern coast of the Adriatic and looked favourably on Hannibal's idea of an Italian confederacy presided over by Capua. Once the Romans found out about the treaty, however, their navy prevented Philip from landing in Sicily. They also attacked his allies in mainland Greece. A few years later they made an alliance with the Aetolian League, a loose confederation of states dominating central Greece that sought to form a buffer against Macedonian expansionism. It was, incidentally, the first alliance that Rome had made in the eastern Mediterranean. The fact that the Macedonians and Aetolians were on different sides in the Second Punic War was typical of the way rival Greeks sought to exploit political crises to their own advantage, though we should note that the Aetolians had been resisting the Macedonians long before they were threatened by Rome. The First Macedonian War would drag on till 205, in which year the Romans concluded a peace with Philip at Phoenice (modern Finiq in Albania). However, little came of Carthage's alliance with Philip in the long run and it had a negligible impact on the course of the war.

Hannibal made yet another unsuccessful attempt to take Nola in 214. He then ordered Hanno son of Bomilcar to advance north from

Fig. 8. Philip V of Macedon. Silver coin, 221-179 BC.

Bruttium and join him in Campania. At Beneventum (modern Benevento) in Samnium Hanno was defeated, however, and his army almost completely destroyed. It was a stunning blow to Hannibal's hopes. Thwarted in his attempt to acquire a naval base in Campania, Hannibal marched north to winter in the Apulian town of Salapia. Once he departed, Fabius and Marcellus seized the small town of Casilinum, three miles to the north of ancient Capua, which it had taken Hannibal months to starve into submission. At the same time Syphax, king of a Numidian tribe called the Masaesylii, revolted from Carthage and concluded an alliance with the Scipios in Spain.

The Romans had come back from the grave. In 213 they raised an army of 20 legions, nearly 100,000 men, making their full complement, counting the allied contingent, 200,000. They stationed two in Sicily, two in Sardinia, two in Cisalpine Gaul (to prevent Hasdrubal from bringing reinforcements to his brother via Spain), one in

Picenum, two in Spain, and two in Rome to serve as a garrison in the event of a siege. They sent the remaining nine into the field to pin Hannibal down, though there was no intention even now to face him in pitched battle. Appian claims that Hannibal burnt alive the wife and children of a certain Dasius of Arpi, who had brought his city over to the Romans after it had previously been allied to the Carthaginians (7.31). The anecdote may well be true. If so, it perhaps reveals a measure of desperation on Hannibal's part.

Events in southern Italy and Sicily dominated 212. A group of aristocrats in the Greek city of Tarentum in the heel of Italy (modern Taranto) seized power and revolted from Rome. Though the Romans managed to hold on to the acropolis, Hannibal succeeded in capturing the lower town by persuading the citizens to drag their warships through the streets to break the Roman blockade – yet another impressive instance of lateral thinking on his part. The Greek cities of Metapontum (modern Metaponto), Thurii (Sibari), and Heraclea (Policoro) fell to the Carthaginians. The only city to resist was Rhegium (modern Reggio di Calabria). Meanwhile in Spain the Scipios captured Tarraco (Tarragona).

The Romans now recaptured Syracuse. Legend has it that the reason why the siege took so long was that the mathematician and scientist Archimedes was among its defenders. What we know best about Archimedes is how he discovered the principle of buoyancy while lying in a tub in a public bath house. The story goes that after solving the problem, he jumped out of the tub and ran down the street naked, shouting '*Eurêka, eurêka!*' – 'I've found it, I've found it!' But Archimedes also excelled in applied science and devised a number of marvellous machines, as Plutarch indicates (*Marcellus* 15.1-3):

> [During the siege of Syracuse] Archimedes fired all manner of missiles and immense stones that landed with terrific noise and violence .... Simultaneously long poles came out of the walls over the ships and

sank some of them by virtue of great weights, which they dropped on top of them from a height. Other ships were lifted into the air by an iron hand or beak in the shape of a crane's beak, and after being hoisted up by the prow … they were hurled to the bottom of the ocean.

Plutarch was writing three centuries after the event and his account may well have been 'sexed up' to show how Greek inventiveness staved off the might of Rome for two years. He offers three versions of the scientist's death. The most colourful is that he was working on a mathematical problem when a Roman soldier ordered him to accompany him to his boss Marcellus. When Archimedes protested that he wanted to solve the problem first, the soldier ran him through with his sword.

Six legions now began besieging Capua with the intention of starving the city into submission, a previous attempt to take the city by storm having failed. The inhabitants appealed to Hannibal, who attempted unsuccessfully to raise the siege. So instead he sought to lure the Romans away from Capua by marching on Rome. He advanced as far as the Colline Gate with 2,000 cavalry. Fear gripped the population. The cry inside the city went up, '*Hannibal ad portas!*', 'Hannibal is at the gates!'. Hannibal did not, however, attempt to lay siege to Rome – a wise decision given the fact that it was garrisoned by perhaps 20,000 men. He merely laid waste to the countryside. His strategy succeeded. In response to the perceived threat, the consul Gnaeus Fulvius Centumalus (or perhaps the proconsul Quintus Fulvius Flaccus) left Capua and marched to the relief of Rome with 15,000 picked infantry and 1,000 cavalry. Though the Romans encamped outside the walls of their city, neither side offered battle, and in the end the march was a futile gesture on Hannibal's part. Livy recounts the patriotic story that the land on which he pitched camp, about seven miles from the city, was sold for its full market price while he was there – stirring proof of the populace's confidence in Rome's invincibility (26.11.6).

Fig. 9. Sixteenth-century (?) copy of a (probably) third-century AD
Roman mosaic depicting the death of Archimedes.

To avoid being trapped between the Roman garrison and Fulvius'
returning army, Hannibal marched south, leaving the Capuans to
their fate. He also had to abandon the Samnite towns in which he had
placed his garrisons. Shortly afterwards the Capuans surrendered
unconditionally, though many of them had committed suicide beforehand either by taking poison or by falling on their swords.
Dozens were now executed and the rest of the population was sold
into slavery. The town was not destroyed but its territory, which was
among the most fertile in Italy, was declared *ager publicus* (public
land) and henceforth administered by the Romans. It was a grim
warning to any of their other allies who might be tempted to defect
to the Carthaginians. For the remainder of his campaign Hannibal
would largely confine his activity to the south coast of Italy and
Bruttium.

101

Towards the end of 211 Hasdrubal son of Gisgo and Hannibal's brother Mago, assisted by the Massylian Numidians under their king Masinissa, defeated and killed both Gnaeus and Publius Scipio. It was a sad end to their seven highly successful years in Spain, during which they had consistently kept the pressure up on Carthage. The following year the command in Spain was transferred to the younger Publius Cornelius Scipio. Aged only 25, he was the first Roman to be appointed to a position that carried *imperium* (literally 'supreme power', including the entitlement to a generalship in war) without having previously held the office of consul or praetor. To be promoted to this rank at such an early age required sedulous and aggressive electioneering. Livy reports the legend, doubtless propagated, if not invented, and never denied, by the Cornelian family, that Publius was the offspring of a monstrous serpent (26.19.7-9). The legend was clearly intended to create an aura around him. His meteoric rise foreshadowed developments in the Late Republic when generals like Pompey and Caesar, who possessed untrammelled military authority as well as gigantic egos, acquired what were in effect private armies and held the state to ransom. Yet despite his youthfulness, Publius was already battle-hardened, having fought at the Ticinus, the Trebbia and at Cannae. He therefore knew Hannibal well and was studied in the tactics he employed. His father's defeat and death at the hands of Hannibal's brother may well have added fuel to these ambitions.

Scipio took Carthago Nova after a siege lasting only one day. The town had been very inadequately defended – a serious lapse on Hannibal's part, if indeed he was still in control of affairs in Spain, which seems doubtful at this point. Even so, Carthage was still able to mount an expedition to reconquer Sicily. In 209, however, Fabius Maximus took Tarentum by means of a ruse. Hannibal is said to have commented afterwards, 'So the Romans also have a Hannibal. We have lost Tarentum the same way that we took it.' Plutarch claims that now for the first time he conceded to his friends that he saw no hope of taking Italy with his existing forces (*Fabius* 23.1). Agrigentum (modern Agrigento), a city on the southeastern coast of Sicily, also fell to the Romans. The Carthaginians no longer had a military presence in Sicily.

Though Hannibal's armies had succeeded in ambushing Gnaeus Fulvius Flaccus at Herdonea (modern Ordona) in Apulia and in slaughtering several thousand of his men in 210, Salapia reverted to the Romans. The following year, however, twelve of the 30 Latin colonies refused to contribute their quotas of men to the Roman army. Though they were not actively disloyal and though the remaining eighteen colonies agreed to make up the shortfall, their resistance was a strong indication of the strain that the war was imposing on Rome's most favoured allies. To justify their act of defiance, the recalcitrants extravagantly complained that serving in the Roman army was a worse fate than being taken prisoner by Hannibal (Livy 27.9.3).

The following year Hannibal ambushed both consuls, Marcus Claudius Marcellus and Titus Quinctius Crispinus, while they were pitching camp near Venusia (modern Venosa). Marcellus, who for once had been recklessly incautious, was among the dead. He was 60 years old. Hannibal, who is reported as saying that he admired 'Fabius as a teacher, but Marcellus as an adversary', cremated his body and sent the ashes to his son (Plutarch, *Marcellus* 9.4). He then attempted to send a message to the inhabitants of Salapia in Marcellus' name sealed with his ring, hoping to trick them into receiving him into their city. However, Crispinus forestalled him by alerting them to the fact that the ring was in Hannibal's possession.

Though Scipio had defeated Hasdrubal in Spain, he failed to prevent him from setting forth to join his brother in Italy in 207. It is strange that Hasdrubal had not set out in 211, as soon as Gnaeus and Publius Scipio had been killed, and equally strange that he did not now transport his forces by sea. The decision that he should journey overland was presumably taken by Hannibal, and it proved disastrous. There is no indication that there was any pre-arranged plan between the two brothers, other than to join forces as best they could. Hasdrubal arrived in the Po Valley around May.

Though he had proceeded more rapidly than the Romans had expected, Hasdrubal lost time besieging Placentia (modern Piacenza). This was a major tactical error, as it gave the Romans time to dispatch one of their consular armies under Gaius Claudius Nero to keep an eye on Hannibal in the south, and the other under Marcus Livius Salinator to observe Hasdrubal in the north. The Romans succeeded in intercepting a message that Hasdrubal sent to Hannibal, in which he suggested that they meet up in Umbria. The fact that their line of communication was so fragile further exposes the fatal inadequacy of Hannibal's preparations.

Livius and Nero joined forces, and Hasdrubal was defeated and killed at the River Metaurus (not far from Rimini). About 10,000 Carthaginians and Gauls fell in the battle, compared with only 2,000 Romans. The grisly story is told that Nero ordered Hasdrubal's head to be tossed unceremoniously into Hannibal's camp. The joy of the Romans was, understandably, unbounded. In Polybius' words, 'It was as if Hannibal, whom they had dreaded so much up till now, was no longer in Italy' (11.3.6). Hannibal was more isolated than ever before and is reported to have remarked ominously that he 'recognised the destiny of Carthage' (Livy 27.51).

Hannibal did not offer battle in 206, allegedly because of grief for his brother – 'a loss not only to his country but also to him personally as well', as Livy reports (28.12.1) – and the Romans were content to leave him be. It is at this point that Livy delivers his encomium on Hannibal, claiming that he was 'more wonderful when facing adversity than he was when enjoying success'. He then goes on to praise him for holding together a motley assortment of races and religions, who 'never quarrelled and never mutinied against their general, though their pay was often lacking and the food to feed them was often insufficient'. All Lucania now submitted to Rome. Scipio won a decisive victory over Hasdrubal son of Gisgo at Ilipa (Alcalá del Rio) near Seville, using a plan that derived in part from Cannae. As a result Hasdrubal was forced to withdraw to Gades.

Gades, the last Carthaginian possession in Spain, fell to the Romans the next year and Hasdrubal returned to Africa. Now, too, Philip V made peace with the Romans. Though Macedon retained its independence, hostilities would resume shortly after Carthage's defeat, ending ultimately in its eclipse. The Carthaginian Senate made one final attempt to bolster Hannibal's flagging campaign by dispatching his brother Mago to Italy with a force of 30 ships and 15,000 men. Mago landed in Liguria near Genua (modern Genoa), made a treaty with a local tribe known as the Ingauni, and held out for two years, trying to discomfit the Romans in north Italy. It is unclear what his long-term goal was, however, or why he landed 600 miles from his brother, since the latter lacked either the resources or the mobility to march north. Once again we have to question Hannibal's overall grasp of strategy.

Hannibal now engraved the bilingual text in Greek and Punic listing his achievements in the temple of Juno Lacinia – 'the memorial to a huge ambition', as Lancel (*Hannibal* [Oxford 1998] 156) aptly phrased it. It is unclear, yet again, why he did not throw in the towel at this point and offer peace terms to the Romans. Though quitting was not in his nature, his last act of defiance, confined within the toe of Italy for three more years, would cost Carthage dear and give Rome time to prepare its assault on Africa. It is also perplexing why he did not try to extend the theatre of action by carrying the war into Sicily.

Even at this late stage in the war, however, the Romans remained jittery. To try to allay their fears, they introduced the cult of the goddess Cybele, otherwise known as the *Magna Mater*, the mother of all things, from Pessinus (modern Balihisar) in Turkey in response to

Fig. 10. Doric column belonging to the temple of Juno
Lacinia at Cape Colonna, where Hannibal set up an
inscription recording his achievements in 206 BC.

a prophecy in the Sibylline Books. The goddess had manifested
herself on Mount Ida as a meteorite and it was in this form that she
now entered Rome. According to tradition the ship that was transporting her ran aground on the banks of the River Tiber. A Roman
matron named Claudia Quinta, accused of adultery, pulled the ship
free, and in so doing proved herself guiltless of the charge. Livy tells
us that the Romans introduced the goddess 'in order to gain all the

106

sooner the victory which the fates, the omens and the oracles forecast' (29.10.8). But they were also eager to enlist the support of the kingdom of Pergamum, under whose auspices the cult now entered Rome, hoping that its king, Attalus, would 'do all he could in the interests of the Roman people', even though it is unclear what kind of help was envisaged from such a distant ally. The introduction of Cybele is highly expressive of the degree to which the Romans yearned for release from their tormentor. Their psychological resolve was close to breaking point.

In the spring of 204, against the advice of the elderly Fabius Maximus, the Romans finally took the war into Africa. Scipio, who had been appointed consul the previous year, was assigned Sicily as his province with permission to invade Africa. After completing his preparations for the invasion, he landed near Utica, which he began unsuccessfully to besiege. His failure no doubt alerted him to the fact that he would not be able to take Carthage by siege. The following year, however, he won a victory over the Carthaginians and their Numidian allies at Campi Magni (Great Plains), 75 miles to the west of Carthage. He succeeded in capturing Syphax, the Numidian king of the Masaesylii, who had allied himself to Carthage. The rival Numidian king Masinissa now switched sides and allied himself to Scipio. Hannibal's Italian campaign was becoming increasingly irrelevant to the outcome of the war.

Hannibal's brother Mago was defeated near Mediolanum (Milan) and ordered by the Carthaginian Senate to return to Africa. In the course of the battle, however, he sustained a serious wound in the thigh and died on the way home. Soon afterwards the same order was relayed to Hannibal. Livy reports that after the emissaries had delivered their message, he commented bitterly, 'It is not the Roman people whom Hannibal defeated in battle so many times and put to flight who have conquered Hannibal, but the malice and envy of the Carthaginians' (30.20.3-4). He added, 'It will not be Scipio who will gleefully rejoice over this shameful return of mine, so much as Hanno [his political enemy in the Carthaginian Senate, quite possibly deceased by now], who, unable to achieve his goal any other way, has brought down my family by bringing down Carthage.' Though these words are no doubt fabricated, Hannibal would not have been far from the mark in ascribing his failure in part to the lacklustre support he'd received from a bitterly divided Senate. At the same time, it clearly served his interests to exaggerate the Senate's failure in order to downplay the fatal weaknesses in his military strategy.

Hannibal embarked for Africa at Croton (modern Crotone). Both his brothers were dead and few of the men who had set out from Spain fifteen years earlier could still have been alive. From the winter of 212-211 onwards, with just one possible exception, he had retreated to the extreme south of Italy at the end of each campaigning season. This in itself had been a tacit acknowledgement of the ineffectiveness of each campaigning season. The wonder is that he did not abandon the expedition earlier, instead of waiting to be recalled by the Senate. The likelihood is that he simply did not have an exit strategy.

As the Senate had failed to provide him with sufficient transport ships, he was forced to build many more. He even had to slaughter his horses to prevent them from falling into enemy hands. Classical historians saw this final, very public announcement of his failure as testing his humanity to the limit. Livy alleges that he massacred – inside the sanctuary of Juno Lacinia no less – those Italians in his army who refused to accompany him back to Africa (30.20.6). Diodorus Siculus repeats this story and puts the total number slaughtered at 20,000, along with 3,000 horses and 'innumerable' pack animals (27.9). He further darkens this picture of a ruthless megalomaniac made to face the ruin of his life's ambition by reporting that on Hannibal's return to Africa he slew 'in a fit of rage' 4,000 cavalry, who, after the defeat of Syphax at Campi Magni, had deserted to his Numidian opponent Masinissa (27.10). Both allegations are of dubious veracity.

The Carthaginian Senate now sent an emissary to the Romans to sue for peace, putting all the blame for the war on Hannibal and claiming that he had acted independently of their wishes (Livy 30.16.5). In response Scipio demanded that the Carthaginians leave Italy, abandon their claim to Spain and to all the islands between Spain and Africa, hand over all but 20 of their warships, pay an indemnity of 5,000 talents, and provide Rome with an abundance of grain. A provisional agreement was struck between the two sides. The more wary of his countrymen would have been right in suspecting that the Carthaginians made the offer simply to buy time until Hannibal returned home. He was still *the* man.

9

The Coda

The last twenty years of Hannibal's life can justly be considered a coda only because our sources are so deficient. Were those sources richer, our portrait would be so much livelier, as our subject, far from meekly accepting his lot in life, underwent transformation. The title of this chapter is a judgement on those sources, not on Hannibal himself, whose energy and ambition – remarkably – remained undimmed.

Hannibal returned to Africa with 15,000-20,000 men and disem-

barked at Leptis Minor (modern Lemta), about 100 miles south of Carthage. He may well have decided that it was unwise to return home at this juncture. This was, quite possibly, the first time he had set foot on the African continent since accompanying his father to Spain aged nine. He was now 43 or 44. It can hardly have felt much like a homecoming. Everything, even the landscape, must have seemed strange. We hear nothing about his wife Imilce and do not know what kind of reception he received. Though he was still the commander-in-chief, his authority must have been considerably reduced. Even so, there were many Carthaginians who saw his return to Africa as their salvation, and this would surely stiffen their resolve for the conflict that lay ahead. Scipio, as we saw, had arrived on the continent the previous year and was based near Utica. Hannibal unsuccessfully attempted to intercept him as he was heading up the Medjerda Valley and then prepared to winter near Hadrumentum (modern Sousse), a coastal city about 80 miles south of Carthage.

In the early spring of 202 Carthage violated its agreement with Rome by attacking some supply ships that had beached near Carthage. Scipio responded by devastating a number of towns in the Medjerda Valley and enslaving their populations. He continued plundering the region for six more months. The Carthaginian Senate hastily sent a delegation to Hannibal, urging him to attack the enemy without delay. Polybius tells us that he curtly informed its members that they should 'attend to other matters and leave him to look after this one' (15.5.2), and that he would himself choose the best moment to fight. The fact is that he needed to increase the size of his army. He eventually left Hadrumentum in the early autumn and marched to Zama, a town five days' march west of Carthage, which was close to the modern Tunisio-Algerian border (15.5.3).

On arrival at Zama in October, Hannibal sent three scouts to spy upon the enemy, but they were discovered and handed over to Scipio. Confident of the superiority of his forces, Scipio obligingly gave them

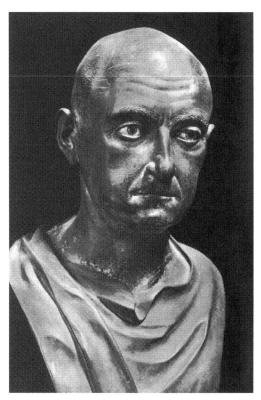

Fig. 11. Bronze bust possibly of the aged Publius
Scipio Africanus, victor at Zama.

a conducted tour of his camp before dispatching them back to
Hannibal. Hannibal now requested a meeting with Scipio, who was
encamped outside a town called variously either Magaron or Narag-
gara (Polybius 15.6-8; Livy 30.29.5-31.10). He was no doubt curious
to meet his adversary, but he may also have sensed that he was facing
almost certain defeat and needed to strike a deal with the Romans.
He had probably learnt that Masinissa was due to arrive in the Roman
camp with 6,000 Numidian infantry and 4,000 cavalry. Just before
the meeting took place Hannibal moved camp.

9. The Coda

The meeting took place with both men communicating through interpreters. Hannibal allegedly spoke of the fickleness of Fortune, pointing to the example of his own career, and suggested that Carthage should give up all its possessions outside Africa, including Spain, Sicily, Sardinia, and the Balearic Islands, on the condition that it could retain its fleet. It can hardly have seemed an attractive offer to Scipio, being less favourable than the terms that Carthage had broken back in the spring. Scipio refused outright and declined to make a counter-offer.

The exact site of the battle is unknown, but it was about four miles west of Zama. Both Polybius and Livy provide an account, but Polybius' is likely to be the more reliable because he was acquainted with Caius Laelius, who had been in charge of one of the Roman cavalry wings. Polybius maintained that the outcome of the battle shaped the future course of Mediterranean history – or 'world history', as he called it, and this is hardly an exaggeration. The political and cultural landscape of the ancient Mediterranean would shift for all time. 'The Carthaginians,' he wrote (15.9.2), 'were fighting for their very survival and for possession of Africa, whereas the Romans were fighting for empire and world dominion.'

The site of the battlefield remains a matter for conjecture. Though the encounter did not actually take place at Zama, that is the name by which it is known, owing to an error on the part of the biographer Nepos. Hannibal's army probably numbered 36,000 infantry, 4,000 cavalry, and 80 battle elephants (many more, incidentally, than he had had during his Italian campaign). Scipio, with Masinissa's forces, probably had about 29,000 infantry and 6,000 cavalry under his command. Many of Scipio's men had lost their fathers at Cannae, so they had a personal score to settle. Others, who were veterans of the campaign in Spain, owed a very strong allegiance to their general. It was they who comprised the *triarii*, the third line of troops according to the literal meaning of the word. They were the toughest and most experienced of his legionaries.

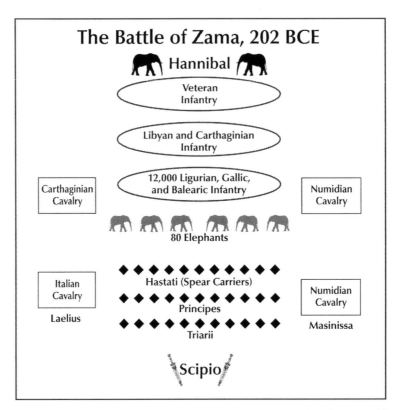

Hannibal set great store by his elephants, hoping that they would trample over the Roman infantry. However, Scipio, who had learned a trick or two from his adversary over the years, neutralised their effectiveness by opening up lanes in his ranks through which the animals charged harmlessly and/or by driving them off to the flanks so that they lumbered into the Carthaginian cavalry. After the elephants had passed through, the Roman lines quickly closed again. It seems likely that their first line defeated Hannibal's first and second lines. The remnant from these two lines then joined the wings of the third line, which was composed of Hannibal's veterans from Italy. A ferocious struggle ensued, lasting several hours. The tide eventually

114

Fig. 12. 'The Battle of Zama' by Paul Henri Motte, *c.* 1890.

turned when the Roman and Numidian cavalry under Laelius and Masinissa respectively, after chasing their opponents from the field, charged into the rear of Hannibal's infantry lines, whereupon his army more or less disintegrated. Hannibal fled the battlefield on horseback. It was perhaps the only time in his life when his spirit broke. He did not draw rein until he arrived back at Hadrumentum, some 120 miles away. The ride had taken him two days. In effect the Hannibalic War had ended.

Concluding his account of the battle, Polybius states that it merely confirmed the truth of the Greek proverb, 'A brave man meets one stronger than himself' (15.16.6), meaning that Hannibal had been outclassed by his opponent. It is important to emphasise, however, that the outcome of the battle was by no means a foregone conclusion. True, Hannibal's tactics were hardly inspired and for once he seems to have had no surprises up his sleeve. Even so, Scipio was heavily outnumbered in terms of his infantry and there's no knowing which side might have won, had not the Roman and Numidian cavalry returned at the exact moment they did, though conceivably the timing of their return may have been part of Scipio's plan. According to Polybius, the Romans lost a mere 1,500 men, whereas the Carthaginian casualties exceeded 20,000, with an equal number of men being taken prisoner (15.14.9). It was in short a complete rout.

Livy states that the Senate summoned Hannibal to Carthage, where he admitted that he'd been defeated 'not only in battle but also in the war' (30.35.10-11). One cannot help wondering what it must have been like to enter the city in such circumstances and after so many years. How did his countrymen greet him? And what mood was the Senate in? Whatever the immediate reaction to his return, Hannibal's reputation was high in future years, as we know from the fact that a large gathering of people used to collect outside his house every day to pay their respects (Livy 33.48.9).

Following Hannibal's advice, Carthage surrendered in 201. Though the terms were more severe than those proposed in 203, they did not differ greatly from those that Hannibal had offered before the battle. Although the Carthaginians retained their independence, they had to acknowledge the autonomy of the previously subjected kingdom of Numidia. They were also required to pay an indemnity of 5,000 talents, which was to be handed over in 50 yearly instalments. (This sum was later raised to 10,000.) They had to give up all their elephants and all but ten of their warships. Scipio ordered the rest of their fleet, some 500 ships in all, to be burnt at sea without warning – a striking example of 'punishment by spectacle' that was intended both to symbolise as well as to enforce Carthage's eclipse as a naval power. Scipio did not, however, demand that the Senate hand over Hannibal, as the Romans had requested before the outbreak of the war. He may well have felt a certain protectiveness towards his former foe and rival, and in some sense his equal.

It is said that when a Carthaginian senator argued against acceptance of the peace terms, Hannibal abruptly pulled him from the platform. After apologising for his behaviour, he proceeded to point out that the terms were far more lenient than the Carthaginians had a right to expect and that they should unanimously approve them without debate. The incident confirms the fact that he had no appetite for further war, and, further, that he was close to the end of his tether. The Senate dutifully complied.

The Romans had won the war despite the fact that many of their allies had gone over to the Carthaginians and despite the fact that they had sustained several crippling defeats. They had prevailed because they had huge reserves of manpower, because the Carthaginians had not sought to win control of the sea lanes, because Hannibal's objective had failed to resonate with Rome's Italian subjects and allies, and because, quite simply, they had refused to entertain the idea of defeat. Their resistance is no less impressive than Hannibal's unwavering determination to destroy them. The essential difference is that he was one and they were many.

It must have taken terrific guts on Hannibal's part to face his political enemies. Given the severity with which the Carthaginians customarily punished their failed generals, it is somewhat surprising that there was no move to have him executed for treason. This was due largely to the popular support that he commanded as a war hero. He had been an inspiration to the Carthaginian people for over a generation, and his defeat, so far as we can tell, seems not to have diminished the aura he possessed in their eyes. Perhaps, as some modern historians have suggested, Scipio intervened with the Carthaginian Senate on his behalf, as he did later with the Roman Senate (see below). It would after all have been in his interests to laud his enemy's ability and advocate leniency towards him.

Livy tells us that the Carthaginian Senators were so devastated when the first payment of the indemnity became due that they all burst into tears – all, that is, except Hannibal, who 'seemed to be laughing' (30.44.4-11). On being reprimanded for his behaviour,

Hannibal commented that his laughter was that of a man almost driven insane by misfortune. He then chided them as follows: 'The time to weep was when our arms were stripped from us, when our fleet was burnt, and when the right to wage war was taken away from us.' They were concerned not about the fate of Carthage, he went on to say, but about having to dig into their coffers to pay the tribute. Once again he cowed them into silence. Whether the anecdote is true or not, it is not beyond the bounds of possibility that it was Hannibal who took the lead in preventing Carthage's defeat from engulfing the very structures of its republic. If so, he had lost none of his powers to inspire.

Hannibal's life now slips increasingly into the shadows. Little is recorded of him between 200 and 197, though Nepos states that he retained his military command (*Hannibal* 7.1). Very likely there was no one to replace him. We do not even know whether he resided in Carthage during these years. According to Aurelius Victor, a Roman historian writing in the late fourth century AD, he ordered his veterans to plant olive trees to prevent idleness from undermining their discipline (*On the Caesars* 37.3). If the story is true, he may have been calculating that the exercise would help to reduce Carthage's indebtedness, though it would have taken about twenty years for the trees to produce a decent crop.

In 196 Hannibal was elected suffete – a position similar to that of consul. The name of his colleague is not preserved. It would be fascinating to know how Hannibal adjusted to civilian life, and to what extent he succeeded in conforming to the conventions of domestic politics after having held a military command for twenty years. It must have entailed a sea change of personality, at least on the outside. There were surely many occasions when he fumed at the tedious and self-serving manner in which the Senate conducted its business. What is evident, however, is that he showed remarkable energy, astuteness and integrity in seeking to reform the legislature and improve the city's finances. He must have had a number of

Fig. 13. Hannibal being crowned as head of government in Carthage after the city had surrendered to Rome, from an edition of Livy's *History* translated into French, *c.* 1410.

political allies, the majority no doubt traditional supporters of the Barcid clan. Though he seems to have adopted what we would call today a populist agenda, and though Livy claims that he was working for 'the public good' (33.46.8), he may well have been primarily motivated by animosity towards members of the anti-Barcid faction – those, in other words, who had been antagonistic to him during his long years in Spain.

He began his year in office by attacking 'the class of judges' (*ordo iudicum*), specifically by authorising the arrest of a financial officer whom he accused of 'insolence'. Bypassing the Senate and appealing directly to the popular assembly, he introduced a law requiring that the term of office for judges in the Court of 104 be limited to one year. On the economic side he stabilized the revenues accruing to the state from both agriculture and harbour dues by enforcing a stricter code of taxation. He even claimed that the money that had been embezzled by Carthage's fat cats was equal to the size of the indemnity that the state owed to the Romans. This was not the way to win friends and influence people. As a result of his initiatives, his political enemies wrote repeatedly to the Romans, accusing him of conspiring with persons hostile to Rome. They even accused him of conspiring with the Seleucid king Antiochus III the Great, whose vast kingdom, a portion of the empire once governed by Alexander the Great, incorporated Syria and Mesopotamia. The charge, though true later, was almost certainly a fabrication at this date.

Meanwhile the Roman Senate debated what to do with Hannibal. Scipio argued that it was 'beneath the dignity of the Roman people to give their names in agreement (*subscribere*) to the animosities of Hannibal's accusers' (Livy 33.47.4). His advice failed to persuade his colleagues, however, many of whom were furious at him for having introduced financial reforms that had rescued Carthage from insolvency. Soon after Hannibal had completed his term of office as suffete, a three-man Roman delegation arrived in Carthage ostensibly to settle outstanding issues between the Carthaginians and the Numidian king Masinissa, but with the added task of investigating charges of conspiracy that his opponents brought against him.

Rightly suspecting that the true purpose of the delegation was to demand his arrest, Hannibal escaped to a fortification that he owned in the coastal strip known as Byzacium not far from Carthage. Only two companions, both ignorant of his plan, accompanied him on his flight (Livy 33.47.10). From Byzacium he sailed to the Cercinna islands (modern Kerkennah), off the east coast of Tunisia, where 'a crowd of people came to greet him' – further evidence of his enduring celebrity status (Livy 33.48.3). He managed to evade arrest by the

HANNIBAL'S WANDERINGS

crew of some Carthaginian ships that happened to be in the harbour by claiming he was on a diplomatic mission to Tyre. He also requested – lateral thinking yet again – the loan of their sails for protection from the glare of the sun at a banquet that he was hosting and to which they were invited. Then in the middle of the night he secretly weighed anchor, secure in the knowledge that he was safe from pursuit. He sailed to the Phoenician city of Tyre on the Lebanese coast, where he was cordially received by a group known as the founders of Carthage 'as a man distinguished by every kind of honour' (Livy 33.49.5). Meanwhile back home the Carthaginian Senate declared him an enemy of the state and ordered that his house be burnt down – a petty gesture that was indicative of their mean-spiritedness (Livy 33.47-49; Nepos, *Hannibal* 7; Justin 31.1-2). For the remaining years of his life, Hannibal would be on the run.

After landing at Tyre, Hannibal journeyed to Antioch on the Orontes River (near modern Antakya in Turkey), where he was granted an audience by the son of Antiochus III. He eventually caught up with the king at Ephesus and offered him his services in any future engagement with Rome. He apparently remained in

Fig. 14. Antiochus III the Great. Silver coin, 223-187 BC.

Ephesus until 192. The previous year, when a Roman delegation was visiting Antiochus, a certain Publius Villius Tappulus tried to in-criminate him by holding frequent assignations with him (Livy 35.14.1-4). Nepos reports that Hannibal sought to counter the charge that he was cosying up to the Romans by telling Antiochus of the oath of eternal enmity that his father had made him take (*Hanni-bal* 1.2-6).

It is at this point that a fanciful anecdote has been inserted into the record. Livy, who quotes an annalistic historian called Claudius (possibly Quadrigarius), who claims to be 'following' (whatever that means) a Greek historian named Acilius (*fl. c.* 150 BC), reports that Scipio, who was another of the delegates, had an informal meeting with Hannibal (35.14.5; cf. Appian, *Syrian Wars* 10). During the conversation he asked him who was the greatest general of all time. 'Alexander, Pyrrhus and myself third,' Hannibal replied. 'What would you say if you had defeated me?' Scipio persisted. 'Then I'd put myself before Alexander, Pyrrhus, and every other general.' It was a nice compliment that displayed both tact and grace, and it moved

Scipio deeply, we are told. Though the story is almost certainly apocryphal, the implication that the two men had come to develop an appreciation for one another is entirely plausible.

Given the fact that Hannibal no longer had a homeland and was at complete odds with his countrymen, he may have struck Antiochus as something of an eccentric, hell-bent on destroying the world's only superpower no matter what the cost to himself and others. But whatever reservations he might have had, the king was eventually persuaded to take up the struggle, fearing, as Hannibal rightly pointed out, that the Seleucid kingdom was next on Rome's hit list.

Hannibal requested 100 warships, 10,000 infantry and 1,000 cavalry so that he could stir up Carthage and once again invade Italy, though he could hardly have succeeded a second time around with a force that small. In any event Antiochus never granted his request, though he did take him on as a military advisor. In 192 Hannibal accompanied the king to mainland Greece, where he urged him to make an alliance with Rome's former enemy Philip V of Macedon. In 190, however, while accompanying Antiochus' fleet across the Aegean from Syria, he came off worse in a naval battle with the Rhodians close to Side, a city on the southern coast of modern Turkey. In January 189 or thereabouts the Romans, aided by Eumenes II of Pergamum, defeated Antiochus at Magnesia, a town a few miles inland from the northwest coast of Turkey. The king fled further east to Apamea on the Orontes River in Syria, from which he sued for peace. The Romans imposed a heavy indemnity on him. They also ordered him to stay out of Europe and withdraw from all Asia west of the Taurus Mountains (a mountain range in southern Turkey that runs parallel to the Mediterranean coast). Hannibal's Seleucid adventure was over.

We have now reached the point where Hannibal's life fades into myth. Suspecting (again rightly) that the Romans would force Antiochus to hand him over, he fled to Armenia. Or at least this is what

Fig. 15. Prusias I of
Bithynia. Silver coin,
c. 230-182 BC.

both Strabo (11.14.6, p. 528) and Plutarch (*Lucullus* 31) allege.
There, they tell us, he laid the foundations for the city of Artaxata
(modern Artashat), about twenty miles south of Yerevan. The city
was named after Artaxias, the then king of Armenia. From Armenia
Hannibal may have travelled to Gortyn in Crete, though it is possible
we should reverse the order of events and have him travel to Crete
before Armenia. According to Nepos, 'being the shrewdest of men'
(*Hannibal* 9.2), he managed to prevent the sizeable fortune that he
had acquired from falling into the hands of pirates by hiding all his
gold and silver coins in hollow bronze statues. It is somewhat amus-
ing, even touching to think of the old warrior lugging a huge treasure
chest with him everywhere he went.

Both the Armenian and the Cretan adventures are, however,
suspect. The fact is that we do not know for certain what Hannibal
did in the years following Antiochus' defeat. He surfaces again in 187,
offering his services to Prusias I of Bithynia, king of a wealthy region
in northwest Turkey, in his war against Rome's ally Eumenes II of
Pergamum. Nepos tells us that he won a naval battle for Prusias in
the Sea of Marmara by tossing jars containing poisonous snakes onto

Eumenes' ships in a failed attempt to kill the king (*Hannibal* 10.4-11.7). Pliny the Elder also credits him with founding a new city in Bithynia called Prusa (modern Bursa), which, like Artaxata, was named after its king (*Natural History* 5.148). It was around now that Hannibal wrote his 'Letter to the Rhodians', in which he described how in 189 the Roman consul Gnaeus Manlius Volso led an expeditionary force into Anatolia in order to massacre the Galatians for having sided with Antiochus III, even though some of them had remained friendly to Rome (Nepos, *Hannibal* 13.2). The letter was clearly intended as a warning to the Rhodians of the danger of throwing in their lot with an unreliable ally like Rome.

The pathos of Hannibal's sadly reduced circumstances caught the eye of Juvenal (*Satire* 10.160-2), who commented: 'Conquered, he fled into exile and there he sits, both mighty and marvellous, a suppliant at the king's vestibule, until such time as it should please the Bithynian tyrant to stir from his bed.' The Latin word for 'suppliant' is *cliens*, which gives us our word 'client'. It is a technical term for a Roman who is dependent upon a patron (Latin *patronus*) either for livelihood or sustenance. The condition of such persons elicited much sympathy from Juvenal, whose persona in the *Satires* identified closely with Rome's *clientes*.

Even now, however, Hannibal could not let go. He 'had the same view of Italy and was obsessed with the idea of arming the king and training his forces to meet the Romans', as Nepos (*Hannibal* 10.1) tells us. The story goes that Prusias sent some ambassadors to Rome, who inadvertently revealed to the Senate the fact that Hannibal was fighting on their side. The endgame was at hand. In late 183 or early 182 Titus Quinctius Flamininus, one of Rome's most distinguished statesmen and soldiers, arrived in Bithynia and persuaded Prusias that it was in his interests to hand over his famous guest to him. The circumstances of Hannibal's death are minutely described. He had constructed a house on the Bithynian coast at a port town called

Libyssa (the modern port of Diliskelesi in Gebze), about 30 miles east of Istanbul). Plutarch tells us that an oracle had foretold him he would be buried in 'the soil of Libyssa', which he supposedly took to mean Libya (*Flamininus* 20.3). We are somehow expected to believe that Hannibal had failed to notice the similarity between the two names.

On learning that Prusias' soldiers were in the vestibule of his house, Hannibal tried to escape by one of the seven underground tunnels that he had constructed precisely for the purpose of facilitating his getaway, only to discover that they were all guarded. So instead he took poison. Once again Juvenal underscores the pathos of his situation (*Satire* 10.163-6): 'No sword or stone or spear will end the life of him who in former times created such havoc for mankind. The avenger of Cannae and of so much blood – is a ring.'[1]

Hannibal was 62 or 63. According to Livy his last words were, 'Let us now put an end to the great anxiety of the Romans, since they have thought it too tedious to wait for the death of a hated old man ... . This day will surely prove how far the moral standards of the Romans have changed' (39.51.9). He also alleges that Hannibal cursed Prusias for violating the laws of hospitality. The famous last words are surely an invention – who recorded them? – though they mesh with Livy's insistent theme that Roman morality deteriorated over the centuries, reaching its nadir in the period of the Civil War between Caesar and Pompey. Plutarch tells us that the Roman Senate condemned Flamininus for having killed Hannibal 'like a bird that was too old to fly and that had lost its tail feathers' – simply so that their names might be associated together (*Flamininus* 21.1). I should dearly like to believe it capable of such magnanimity.

There is an interesting coda to this coda. It is just conceivable, as Giovanni Brizzi (*Studi di storia annabalica* [Faenza 1984] 101) has

---

[1] The claim that Hannibal owned a ring containing poison is Juvenal's invention.

suggested, that the 'Letter to the Athenians', falsely attributed to Hannibal, was circulated at the time of his death to exploit the widespread grief that this event generated (*Papyrus Hamburg* 129). In it the author reminds the Athenians of Hannibal's illustrious victory at Cannae and prophesies that if they and other Greeks rise up against Rome they will achieve liberation. If the dating is correct, this strongly suggests that the final twelve years of Hannibal's life should not be casually dismissed as a fruitless campaign waged by a superannuated old buffer, who refused to make peace with the political realities of his day. On the contrary, Hannibal may well have been a beacon of hope for the increasingly embattled and fearful Greeks, who understood all too well that the victor in the Second Punic War would not be content 'with the sovereignty of Italy and Sicily' (see below, p. 130).

10

The Unintended Legacy

Hannibal's unintended legacy is all around us. At the beginning of Book 21 of his *History* Livy writes, 'The war which the Carthaginians fought against the Romans under the generalship of Hannibal was the most memorable ever fought.' Though the claim may be somewhat questionable, our world is distinctively post-Hannibalic. It was, moreover, the experience of the Second Punic War that first stimulated the Romans to write a national history. Not without good reason did Polybius choose 220 BC as the year to begin his narrative of Rome's takeover of the Mediterranean.

It is largely due to Hannibal's defeat at Zama that we became the heirs of the Greeks and the Romans. Had Scipio lost, there is no guarantee that the Carthaginians would have incorporated Hellenic culture into their lifeblood in the way the Romans did, notwithstanding the fact that Hellenism had already begun to take root in Hannibal's day. After the fall of Syracuse, Marcellus shipped a vast number of sculptures and other works of art to Rome. Plutarch (*Marcellus* 21.5) says he boasted that it was he who 'had taught the ignorant Romans how to admire and appreciate stunningly beautiful Greek works of art'. Henceforth wealthy Romans competed with one another to acquire these works and by so doing demonstrate their cultural élitism. Next, the assimilation of Greek gods and Greek religious observances, as well as the high regard in which the Romans held the books of Sibylline prophecy and the oracle of Delphi, intensified Rome's indebtedness to Greek culture. Lastly, though

Syracuse's population had escaped enslavement after the city fell, other communities in *Magna Graecia*, Great Greece, i.e. southern Italy and Sicily, were not so fortunate. The population of Agrigentum was enslaved, and possibly that of Tarentum as well, since both of them had at times supported Hannibal in the war. With the influx of slaves into Rome, the Romans now came into contact with the Greeks on a daily basis, albeit in their asymmetrical roles of master and slave. Livius Andronicus, a native of Tarentum and allegedly the first author to adapt a play into Latin from a Greek original, may well have been among their number.

In sum, it was the Hannibalic War which drew the Romans into the Greek orbit as never before and which fostered among intellectuals a desire to own Greek works of art, learn the Greek language, and imitate the Greek way of life. Rome's relationship with the Greek world, though conflicted, is why that world came to shape the way we ourselves understand drama, philosophy, history, medicine, political science, ethnography, aesthetics, and so on. If things had turned out differently, it is possible that Semitic, rather than Graeco-Roman culture might have prevailed throughout the Mediterranean. It is even conceivable that, instead of French, Spanish, Portuguese, Italian and Romanian, various subdivisions of the Semitic tongue would be spoken in Europe today. Taking this counter-factual scenario one step further, it is perhaps questionable whether anti-Semitism would have taken such a vicious hold.

All this presupposes that the Carthaginians would have been able to maintain control over the Mediterranean, which, given the limited size of their citizen body, is by no means a certainty, and further that they would have risen to the challenge of world domination, which, given their tendency towards exclusivity, is highly improbable. Perhaps a more likely scenario is that the Mediterranean would have fallen under the grip of a different power (or set of powers). A further possibility is that some sort of bipolarity might have evolved, with the western Mediterranean falling under the sway of Carthage and the eastern Mediterranean under that of the three Hellenistic power blocs that emerged on the death of Alexander the Great – the Antigonid dynasty that ruled Macedon and Greece, the Ptolemaic that ruled Egypt, and the Seleucid that ruled Syria-Mesopotamia, unopposed in this case by the rising power of Rome.

Arguably Hannibal's greatest legacy was the fact that he left Rome with no serious rival, as was probably evident to most thinking persons at the time. Polybius claims that after the Battle of Lake Trasimene a certain Agelaus of Naupactus issued this warning to his fellow-Greeks (5.104.3): 'It is apparent even to those of us who pay only little attention to affairs of state that, whether the Carthaginians beat the Romans or the Romans beat the Carthaginians, it is not in the least bit likely that the victor will be content with the sovereignty of Italy and Sicily but is certain to come over here [i.e. to mainland Greece] and extend his ambitions and forces beyond the bounds of justice.' And so indeed it proved. A terrible irony thus lies at the core of Hannibal's career, made more terrible on the personal level by virtue of the fact that he lived long enough to see his 'legacy' evolve. Linda-Marie Günther (*Brill's New Pauly* vol. V [Leiden and Boston 2004] col. 1129) writes, 'Hannibal's historical importance lies in the fact that he brought to light to his contemporaries and to later generations the relentlessness of Rome's politics of alliance and expansion, which proved fatal to its enemies.' Relentlessness is the key word. Much of the Iberian peninsula now passed under Roman sway and its inhabitants began to speak Latin. The region became an important source of revenue to the Romans, with the silver mines at Carthago Nova alone producing 25,000 drachmas per day (Polybius 34.9.8-11).

Hannibal's campaign had a lasting effect on the Roman psyche by testing it as it had never been tested before. In a moving passage Livy (22.54.9-10), commenting on Rome's condition after Cannae, writes, 'Two consuls and two consular armies had been destroyed, and there was no longer any Roman camp or any general or any soldier. Hannibal was in control of Apulia, Samnium, and almost the whole of Italy.' In other words, it was by fighting the Carthaginians that the Romans acquired the mental resilience as well as the military skills and discipline to dominate the Mediterranean. At the same time he instilled in Rome a dread of Carthage, coupled with the dread of a possible successor to himself. This was what Marcus Porcius Cato – Cato the Elder or Cato the Censor, as he is known to us – exploited in the years leading up to the Third Punic War nearly half a century later. His famous battle cry, with which he ended all his speeches to the Senate, *Carthago delenda est*, 'Carthage must be destroyed', signalled that Rome and Carthage were locked in a life-and-death struggle. He even went so far as to produce a fig, which he claimed had been picked only three days earlier in Carthage! Cato's scaremongering eventually paid off and Rome declared war on Carthage in 149. Following Rome's victory three years later, the city was burnt and its people prohibited – temporarily, as it turned out – from rebuilding it. However, there is no evidence that Cato ever evoked the name of Hannibal to whip up alarm or indeed that he suggested that a reincarnation of him would one day again torment the Romans.

The destruction of Carthage became the stuff of legend, fuelling the belief, based on no ancient testimony, that the Romans ploughed salt into the site so that nothing should ever grow there again.[1] The anecdote can be traced back to B.L. Hallward's chapter 'The Siege of Carthage' in the *Cambridge Ancient History* vol. VIII (Cambridge 1930), though it perhaps owes its ultimate origins to the German historian Barthold Niebuhr (1776-1831), who claimed – again on no ancient authority – that the Romans ordered a plough to be driven over the ruins of the city. As Lancel (*Carthage: A History* [Oxford, etc.

---

[1] See John Peddie (*Hannibal's War* [Stroud 1977] 204): 'They buried [Carthage] deep in sand and scattered salt upon the site so that nothing should ever grow again where it had stood.'

1995] 428f.) notes, however, excavations carried out by the French archaeological mission in the 1970s proved that the Punic city was not razed to the ground. In fact in some places the remaining walls are two feet in height.

Hannibal's tactical genius forced the Romans to revise their notion of what constituted a military engagement. Previously their battles had been ritual events that took place with due attention to the formalities and, typically, on an open field. The ambush at Lake Trasimene shattered that concept once and for all. Hannibal's victories also revealed the superiority of a tightly disciplined professional army over a citizen militia, which is all that the Romans had at their disposal till then. In addition, the difficulty that they had experienced in implementing an effective and consistent strategy, in part because of their policy of having generals take command on alternate days, had starkly demonstrated the need to appoint a single commander-in-chief.

The loss of life due to the war was staggering. Appian (*Punic Wars* 134) puts the total number of Roman and allied dead 'in battles alone' at 300,000. Though this figure is doubtless an exaggeration, it may not be wildly far from the mark if it includes civilians who died as a result of military action. The war also caused ecological degradation of the Italian countryside on a vast scale, even though the blame for this cannot be laid solely at Hannibal's door. As we have seen, when Fabius Maximus became dictator in 217, he ordered the inhabitants of all the fortified towns within striking distance of Hannibal's forces to move within their walls, burn their homesteads and destroy their crops, so that the enemy would not be able to live off their produce. In 215, when Fabius became consul, he re-issued the same order, backing it up with the threat that his army would devastate the land of anyone who failed to comply. Though the authenticity of this decree has been questioned, there is no obvious reason why Livy, who records it, should have invented it, since it was far from complimentary to the Romans (23.32.14). Appian (*loc. cit.*)

reported that Hannibal also destroyed 400 towns in Italy, and it may be that between them the Romans and Carthaginians destroyed double that number in total. In other words, the modern carbon footprint has its precedent in antiquity – one that is no less catastrophic if we take into account the lives and livelihoods of all those whose homes, fields and fruit trees fell victim to the scorched-earth policy that both sides practised.

Arnold Toynbee (*Hannibal's Legacy* vol. 2 [Oxford 1965] 35) made the bold claim that the consequences of this widespread destruction lasted into the twentieth century. He observed: 'At the time of writing in AD 1962, the marks of *dirus*[2] ('dreadful'; see below, p. 135) Hannibal's presence in southeast Italy during the fifteen years 217-203 BC were still discernible.' This is an extreme instance of an attempt to attach blame for a historical event on a single individual, and few historians or environmentalists would today treat the claim seriously. Even so, Peter Brunt's attempt (*Italian Manpower* [Oxford 1971] 269-77) to minimise the effects of the devastation has not won universal acceptance either.[2] It is entirely plausible, moreover, as Toynbee further claimed, that the large number of dispossessed people who fled from the countryside during the war never returned once hostilities ended. This would have contributed to the demise of the smallholder and to the rise of large estates owned by wealthy landowners, fuelling the social and political unrest that became acute a century later.

Toynbee wrote two thick tomes in which he analysed the military, economic, agricultural, social, religious, administrative and political consequences of the Second Punic War. 'War,' he states in the preface to volume 2 (p. v), 'posthumously avenges the dead on the survivors, and the vanquished on the victors.' No doubt his own experience of

[2] For a rebuttal of Brunt, see T. Cornell, 'The effects of the Hannibalic war on Italy', esp. pp. 104-13 in T. Cornell *et al.* (eds), *The Second Punic War: a Reappraisal* (London 1996).

two world wars had brought him to this sobering conclusion. His over-arching thesis was that Hannibal's 'posthumous victory over Rome', as he calls it, ultimately undid the Republic by speeding up changes, which, though inevitable, now became revolutionary and led inexorably to the establishment of the Augustan Principate. 'Legacy' is a complex notion, whose tentacles, if untended, can spread in any direction, and it needs to be invoked with appropriate caution. The relationship between individual agency and historical process is virtually impossible to disentangle.

11

The Afterlife

As we have seen, Rome's victory over Hannibal was memorialised by the award of the honorific title or *agnomen* 'Africanus' to the architect of that victory on his return to the capital in triumph. The victory did not, however, allay the fear Hannibal had generated, and he remained for at least three centuries a symbol of Roman paranoia. The expression 'Hannibal is at the gates!' became a tag to intimidate disobedient children, much as the English used the name 'Boney' to scare their children during the Napoleonic Wars. At least two poets coupled his name with the adjective *dirus*, meaning 'dreadful, terrifying, abominable', which suggests that this was a stock characterisation (Horace, *Odes* 3.6.36; Juvenal 7.161). What afterlife his name enjoyed in Carthage is entirely unknown.

Rome's struggle with Carthage became the stuff of epic, and no event in its history did more to fire up either the historical or the poetical imagination. It was this war, as we have seen, that prompted the emergence of a nationalistic historiography. The first poet to celebrate the heroism of the Roman people was Gnaeus Naevius (*c.* 270-201), who wrote an epic entitled *The Punic War* in Saturnian metre (a somewhat clumsy metre consisting of six-foot iambics). Although his subject was the First Punic War, the fact that he composed the poem during the Second Punic War gave it an obvious contemporary resonance and relevance. Naevius also wrote at least two tragedies based on Roman history. A generation later (*c.* 180) Quintus Ennius wrote an epic in hexameter verse entitled the *Annales*, whose middle section covered the Second Punic War. It contained the famous tribute to Fabius Maximus, 'One man alone, by delaying, re-established the state' (*unum hominem nobis cunctando rem restituisse*), which Livy quotes with approval (30.26.9).

Ennius' poem remained *the* Roman national epic for nearly two centuries until it was eventually superseded by Virgil's *Aeneid*, which was written in the age of Augustus. Virgil's Dido, the founder and queen of Carthage, whose story is told in Book 4, is Hannibal's spiritual as well as biological ancestor. When Aeneas, its soon-to-be founding father, abandons her under an order from Jupiter to attend to his mission, she instructs her people as follows (here rendered in John Dryden's magnificent translation published in 1697):

> These are my prayers, and this my dying will;
> And you my Tyrians, ev'ry curse fulfil.
> Perpetual hate, and mortal wars proclaim,
> Against the prince, the people, and the name.
> These grateful off'rings on my grave bestow;
> Nor league, nor love, the hostile nations know:
> Now, and from hence in ev'ry future age.
> When rage excites our arms, and strength supplies the rage:
> Rise some avenger of our Libyan blood,
> With fire and sword pursue the perjur'd brood:
> Our arms, our seas, our shores oppos'd to theirs,
> And the same hate descend on all our heirs. (4.621-9)

Dido is consumed with profound hatred for the Roman race, even though that race has not yet come into being. She foresees the birth of Hannibal, even though she cannot identify him by name. By invoking him in the second person, however, it is as if she is using her dark arts to summon him magically into existence generations before his birth. The deep sense of betrayal that she feels as a result of Aeneas' behaviour thus provides not only the motivation but also the precedent for Hannibal's hatred of Rome, while her terrifying curse is the counterpart and the forerunner to the oath that Hamilcar allegedly administered to his son. It is powerful testimony to Hannibal's enduring reputation as Rome's most implacable foe a full century and a half after his death that Virgil could confidently expect his readers to experience a frisson of terror when Dido delivered these lines. That they no doubt obliged was due in part to the fact that they would have identified the Carthaginian queen with Cleopatra VII, queen of Egypt, whose recent liaison with Mark Antony, according to the strident and hyped message of Augustan propaganda, had represented a no less deadly threat to Rome's survival and identity during the civil war between Antony and Octavian. Cleopatra had been accused of threatening to 'orientalise' the empire and move its capital to Alexandria, so Dido was an obvious stand-in.

The Virgilian analogy makes the threat that Hannibal presented to Rome historically determined. It also personalises the conflict by invoking Hannibal in his future incarnation as an avenging spirit. In a stirring passage that celebrates Roman coolness under fire, his great predecessor, the epic poet Lucretius (99-55 BC), had merely instanced Hannibal's assault without mentioning him by name: 'Just as in times past we experienced no anxiety when the Carthaginians were coming to attack us, when the whole world, shattered by the terrifying alarms of war, trembled and shook under the lofty pinnacle of heaven, and when no one knew which side would claim dominion over land and sea', in the same way, he continues, a good Epicurean, who is untroubled by fear, will feel nothing when death draws near (*On the Nature of Things* 3.832-7). Though Lucretius saw the Hannibalic War as the ultimate test of the nation's courage, he refrained from suggesting that Hannibal still functioned as a bogeyman in the nation's febrile imagination.

Nearly a century after Virgil, Silius Italicus (AD 26-102) made Hannibal the leading character in his epic *Punica*, or *The Punic Wars*. Weighing in at over 12,000 lines, *Punica* has been described as the longest poem in the Latin language and the least inspired. Pliny the Elder's judgment – 'executed with more assiduousness than genius' – is no less damning. Silius, who in a sense begins where Virgil leaves off, explicitly presents the Second Punic War as the fulfilment of Dido's curse. He also serves up a big dollop of racist stereotyping by repeated references to Hannibal's *rupta fides* (broken word), *ira* (wrath), and, worse than *ira*, *furor* (ungovernable rage). In sharp contrast, all his Roman characters, including Fabius Maximus, Marcus Marcellus and the younger Scipio, exhibit unwavering fortitude and totally above-the-board decency. Even so, his Hannibal is not entirely without redeeming features. When (unhistorically) a deputation of Carthaginian senators arrives in his camp after the Battle of Lake Trasimene to inquire whether he will consent to the immolation of his infant son in sacrifice to the Punic gods, as Carthaginian tradition demanded after such a spectacular victory (according to the conceit of the poem), he orders that the child be spared so that he can become the 'heir to his military fortune' (*Punica* 4.814). Silius' readers would therefore have concluded that at least in his aversion to human sacrifice Hannibal was a cut above his compatriots, although the sparing of his son also guaranteed that Dido's curse would live on after his death.

Hannibal became a stock figure in the Roman declamatory tradition. In *Satire* 7 the poet Juvenal, who was writing around the turn of the second century AD, notes that teachers of rhetoric require their students to debate 'whether Hannibal should march on Rome after Cannae or whether after the rain and thunder he should cautiously lead his cohorts around it, soaked by the storm' (7.162-4). Then in *Satire* 10 Juvenal declares: 'Put Hannibal in the scales. How many pounds will that outstanding general amount to? This is the man whom Africa could not contain, who added Spain to his empire, who leapt over the Pyrenees ...' (10.147-52). Though Juvenal only mentions Hannibal, his comment could equally apply to any general, so it can and should be seen as a powerful denunciation of all military ambition, including Roman military ambition. Slipping into the historical present, Juvenal continues, 'On your way, you madman, race over the savage Alps so that you can give pleasure to schoolboys and become a subject fit for declamation' (10.166-7). 'Madman' is a terrifying judgement on the futility of all human endeavour, made more terrifying in Hannibal's case by the yawning gap between effort and consequence. Though the observation holds true for all human striving, in Juvenal's eyes Hannibal's life was the classic exemplum of wasted effort. Dr Samuel Johnson transposed this passage in an incomparable couplet in his imitation of *Satire* 10, which he appropriately entitled 'The Vanity of Human Wishes' (dated 1749):

> He left a name, at which the world grew pale,
> To point a moral and adorn a tale.

Juvenal's judgement on failed endeavour was pithily echoed by Robert Frost in his poem entitled 'Hannibal' (1928), quoted above, opposite p. 11. Lastly, in *Satire* 6 Juvenal compares the over-privileged and mollycoddled women of his day with their sturdy no-nonsense forebears, whose hands were roughened by spinning wool 'at the time when Hannibal was near the city and their husbands stood at the Colline Gate' (290f.).

Familiarity with the name and deeds of Hannibal was probably due primarily to the fact that Roman schoolboys grew up reading Livy's account of the Punic Wars, though we should not exclude the possibility that the story of those wars was also transmitted orally. Hannibal's name continued to unnerve at least as late as the end of the first century AD. As we've seen, Silius Italicus, writing in the 60s or 70s AD, constructed his whole epic around the Second Punic War. A decade or two later the Emperor Domitian ordered the execution of a Roman senator on the charge of conspiracy in part for naming two of his slaves Hannibal and Mago. This was surely either a *faux pas* or a joke in poor taste, but the clinically paranoid Domitian, who was hardly noted for his robust sense of humour, interpreted it as evidence of treasonable intent. (A more serious allegation was the fact that the senator in question possessed a horoscope predicting that he would one day become emperor.)

However, by the end of the second century AD, if not before, Hannibal's name had lost its power to chill the Roman heart. Tzetzes, a Byzantine poet and grammarian of the twelfth century, claimed that the Emperor Septimius Severus, who, like Hannibal, came from Africa, made formal peace with the memory of Rome's greatest adversary by covering his tumulus in white marble. The date was probably between AD 193 and 195, nearly four centuries after his death (*Chiliades* 1.803). His motive was no doubt self-interested. Hannibal was, after all, Africa's most famous son and Severus no doubt hoped that some of the glamour would rub off on him. The Elder Pliny had previously informed his readers that the tumulus was located at Libyssa, where Hannibal had committed suicide (*Natural History* 5.148). A pile of stones on a small hill in an industrial complex in Gebze, which now covers the ancient town, is said to mark his grave, but excavations carried out in 1906 by the German archaeologist Theodor Wiegand brought nothing to light.

With the waning of antiquity Hannibal faded from the collective memory, to be revived in the late thirteenth century. This was largely due to the popularity of Livy, who was regarded by the humanists as the greatest of the Roman historians and who by the middle of the sixteenth century had been translated into French, German, Italian and Spanish. The earliest reference to Hannibal is in Dante, who, though he does not mention him by name, speaks of the heap of gold rings that he ordered to be removed from the bodies of Roman senators and knights after the Battle of Cannae, 'as Livy writes, who does not err' (*Inferno* 28.10-12). Early in his career Petrarch (1304-

74) began writing an epic poem in hexameter verse called *Africa*, largely based on Livy's account of the Second Punic War in which Hannibal features prominently, though Petrarch's hero is Scipio, and in *Sonnet* 103 he criticizes Hannibal for 'not knowing how to make good use of his victorious fortune' after Cannae. Scenes from Hannibal's life, many of them imaginative, also feature commonly as illustrations in a number of medieval manuscripts of the fourteenth to sixteenth centuries (see Fig. 13).

The essayist Michel de Montaigne compared Hannibal to Alexander the Great, ascribing to him the same qualities of 'speed, foresight, endurance, self-discipline, subtlety, magnanimity, resolve, and good luck' ('On the most excellent of men'). Montaigne seems, however, to have been ill-acquainted with the facts of his life, for he charges Hannibal with having voluntarily abandoned the war in Italy in order to defend his homeland ('On the uncertainty of our judgement'). In Shakespeare's *Henry VI Part 1* (1591) the Earl of Talbot characterises him as a soldier of principle, unlike 'the witch' Joan of Arc, who 'by fear, not force, like Hannibal, drives back our troops' (Act I Scene 5). In *Measure for Measure* (1604) Elbow, a dull-witted constable, expostulates, 'O thou caitiff .. O thou varlet ... O thou wicked Hannibal' – conceivably a malapropism for 'cannibal' (Act II Scene 1). Since Elbow is a low-life character, the majority of Shakespeare's audience would presumably have been expected to catch the allusion, an indicator that by the beginning of the seventeenth century Hannibal had become a familiar name in England, consequent perhaps upon the publication of the first translation of Livy into English by Philemon Holland in 1600.

The French monarchy of the sixteenth century had a serious penchant for Hannibal. The Battle of Zama featured in the magnificent series of tapestries made for François I between 1532 and 1535. The tapestries, which depicted the exploits of Scipio, were based on cartoons that had been executed by an Italian artist called Giulio

Romano, known in France as Jules Romain (*c.* 1499-1546). Though the original was destroyed in the French Revolution, a copy of the Zama tapestry survives in Madrid. It depicts the moment when Hannibal's elephants advance towards the Roman frontline, only to be repulsed with torches. The composition is highly innovative: it puts the viewer on the same plane as the Roman soldiers, who seek to obstruct the elephants' progress. Henri II, who succeeded François I to the throne in 1547, owned a shield that depicts the Battle of Cannae. Henri identified with the Carthaginians and regarded Hannibal as his spiritual and military ancestor in his war against Charles V of Spain, the Holy Roman Emperor. He believed that Cannae foreshadowed his own future victory over Charles. Very possibly he bore the shield when he dressed in parade armour. Made of steel and embossed with silver and gold, it is thought to be the work of a French goldsmith called Etienne Delaune (*c.* 1519-83). François Girardon (1628-1715), who decorated the palace at Versailles for Louis XIV, owned a bronze bust of Hannibal wearing a breastplate. It was donated to the Louvre but has since disappeared. A bronze bust of seventeenth-century date depicting a curly-haired man wearing a cuirass with a gorgon in the centre that was sold at an auction in 1939 may be this work, though it could also be a portrait of a Roman emperor.

In Jacques-Louis David's *Napoleon crossing the St Bernard Pass* (several versions, 1801-5), which commemorated Napoleon's crossing of the Alps prior to his invasion of Italy in 1800, the names of Hannibal and Charlemagne, generals who had previously undertaken the same feat, are engraved on a rock under the front legs of the First Consul's horse. It was probably Napoleon's idea to add their names, just as it was his desire, we are told, to be portrayed by David as 'calm, mounted on a fiery steed'. The humdrum truth of the matter is that the real Napoleon crossed the Alps mounted on a lowly mule led by a guide.

The so-called Hall of Hannibal in the Capitoline Museum in

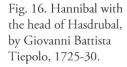

Fig. 16. Hannibal with the head of Hasdrubal, by Giovanni Battista Tiepolo, 1725-30.

Rome includes four frescoes traditionally attributed to Jacopo Ripanda that depict scenes from the Punic Wars. In one, entitled *Hannibal in Italy* (1508-9), Hannibal, seated on an elephant and in the dress of an oriental potentate, towers majestically above his army as he advances calmly against a walled town that could be Rome (Fig. 4, p. 67). Giovanni Battista Tiepolo's *Hannibal sees the Head of Hasdrubal* (1725-30) in the Kunsthistorisches Museum of Vienna has its subject turn away from the grisly sight of his decapitated brother's head, while his gaze remains irresistibly fixed upon it (Fig. 16).

Hannibal

In 1812, in the immediate aftermath of Napoleon's disastrous retreat from Moscow, J.M.W. Turner painted the Tate Gallery's *Hannibal Crossing the Alps.* Turner concentrated on the turmoil of Hannibal's army, which has been caught in a raging tempest. In the foreground we dimly discern a scene of rape, plunder, and slaughter. Hannibal, pathetically minute in the middle distance and mounted on an elephant, is proceeding towards the Po Valley, which lies below him. Both the perspective, the scene and the gloomy tonality indicate that his mighty enterprise is doomed to failure. Turner subsequently painted two other paintings with Carthage as their theme: *Dido Building Carthage* (1815) and *The Decline of the Carthaginian Empire* (1817), also both in the Tate Gallery. A painting by Nicolas Poussin entitled *Hannibal Crossing the Alps* (1626-7), currently on long-term loan to the Frick Collection in New York, depicts an absurdly small Hannibal astride a gigantic elephant. It, too, albeit far less dramatically, conveys the idea of grandiose failure. *Hannibal with his Armoured Elephants* (1982), painted with lacquer by the post-Second World War German artist Sigmar Polke, captures something of the turbulent atmosphere of Turner's painting. A single elephant confronts an armoured tank, a horse seems to reel, while a bearded figure (?) watches on.

Military tacticians, including the Duke of Wellington and Napoleon, have revered Hannibal. In *Mémorial de Sainte-Hélène* (Paris 1823, vol. II, ch. 11, p. 338) Napoleon heaps so much praise on him that it almost amounts to fawning idolatry: 'This most daring of all men, perhaps the most astonishing; so bold, so assured, so broad of vision in all things; who at the age of 26 conceives what is scarcely conceivable and carries out what was deemed impossible; who, giving up all communication with his own land, passes through hostile or unknown peoples whom he must attack and conquer ... .' And so forth.

For twentieth-century generals the Battle of Cannae was the gold standard of military engagements, sometimes evoked to invite favourable comparison with their own tactical brilliance. Count Alfred von Schlieffen, German Chief of Staff from 1891 to 1905 and the author of the 'Schlieffen Plan', which in modified form served as German strategy during the First World War, argued that the country could win a war on two fronts even if it was heavily outnumbered by powerful enemies so long as it followed Hannibal's example. Von Schlieffen ordered the writing of a collection of essays under the title of *Cannae*, the first of which is an account of that battle. In 1941, Field Marshal Erwin Rommel, while driving back the British Eighth Army from Libya towards Tobruk in the north African desert, wrote in his diary that 'a new Cannae is being prepared'.[1] Rommel failed to take Tobruk, however, and a more striking parallel is that, like Hannibal, he committed suicide by taking poison, in preference to being brought to trial by Hitler for high treason. Most recently General H. Norman Schwarzkopf claimed that the strategy he implemented in the Gulf War (1991) to destroy Iraq's war-making capacity was based on a study of Cannae.

Hannibal has also inspired distinguished non-combatants. For the schoolboy Sigmund Freud he was a Semitic role model – his 'favourite hero', as he states in *The Interpretation of Dreams* (1900, translated J. Crick [Oxford 1999] 151). 'Hannibal and Rome symbolized to me the opposition between the tenacity of the Jews and the organization of the Catholic Church', he wrote. Freud recalls his father recounting an occasion when 'a Christian' knocked his cap off and ordered him off the pavement. 'What did you do?' the child demanded. 'I stepped into the road and picked my hat up', his father replied. Freud compares his father's submissiveness unfavourably with the oath of vengeance that Hamilcar made his son swear – he actually gets the name wrong and calls Hannibal's father Hasdrubal instead – and declares that 'From that time on Hannibal had a place in my fanta-

---

[1] W. Heckmann, *Rommel's War in Africa* (London 1981) 113, quoted in Goldsworthy, *Cannae* (London 2001) 197.

sies'. Freud also identified with Hannibal in the fact that he made several abortive attempts to visit Rome. He eventually overcame his curious neurotic inhibition, however, and entered the city in 1901.

Understandably 'Annibale' is an unusual Italian name. If thought goes into the choice at all, the name is perhaps bestowed in the hope that the bearer will grow up to be a rebel. The most celebrated son of this name was the great classical painter Annibale Carracci (1560-1609). Hannibal Hamlin, Vice-President of the United States under Abraham Lincoln from 1861 to 1865, perhaps owes his name to assonance. Hannibal Brooks is the name of an English P.O.W. played by Oliver Reed in the film of that name directed by Michael Winner (Scimitar Films 1969). In a nice reversal of history, Reed's Hannibal risks his life after escaping from a German zoo where he has been working in the company of a baby elephant, for which he seeks to find a safe haven in Switzerland. Hannibal Lecter, the fictional serial killer invented by the novelist Thomas Harris, was presumably so christened because his name rhymes with 'cannibal', though the historical Hannibal actually opposed the suggestion that he should accustom his men to eating human flesh while on the march (see above, p. 22). Just a few miles from where I live in upstate New York lies a village called Hannibal, which was first settled in 1802 (population of 502 according to the 2000 census). The name was bestowed upon it by Robert Harpur, who was responsible for many of the classical names that grace towns in the region (Cicero, Ilion, Tully, Utica, etc.). There is also a town named Hannibal in Missouri, founded in 1819, which boasts that it was 'the boyhood home of Samuel Langhorne Clemens – the famous Mark Twain'. There's even a Tunisian television channel known as 'Hannibal TV': Hannibal was and remains Tunisia's most famous son.

Hannibal's reputation for intrepid adventurism remains undimmed. Advertisements for an Australian company known as *Hannibal Safari Equipment*, 'a world leader in the design and production of expedition equipment', bear the logo of an elephant. He and his elephant are, in fact, inseparable in the popular imagination. The gin-based drink known as *Pimm's No. 1* was advertised in 1947 in the UK with a picture of Hannibal on an elephant inspecting his troops. It carried the by-line: 'When Hannibal crossed the Alps he may have been searching for a long drink as good as *Pimm's No. 1*. He was born too early. You are more fortunate, and may on occasion enjoy the Original Gin Sling without bothering to ride an elephant.' Hannibal even gave his name to a now retired robot that was designed for autonomous planetary exploration in the 1990s by Mobot Lab in the USA. His fellow-robots were dubbed Boadicea, Genghis and Attila.

For poets, novelists, film directors, and, I might add, biographers the absence of any documented love interest makes Hannibal's life a hard sell with the public. Sadly history does not link him with the most famous Carthaginian woman of her day, Sophonisba, the daughter of Hasdrubal son of Gisgo, military commander in Spain. Sophonisba, a political pawn who was once betrothed to Masinissa and then at her father's insistence married Syphax, would certainly have made a worthy partner in that she, too, took poison to avoid being paraded in triumph through the streets of Rome. She later acquired the identity of a tragic heroine in both operas and tragedies, as well as featuring prominently in paintings. Silius Italicus was the first to attempt to fill the void in Hannibal's fictional life by giving a minor supporting role to his Iberian wife Imilce. He depicts her not only as a doting and devoted wife, but also as a proto-feminist, as we see from her spirited farewell to her husband before he goes off to war (*Punica* 3.109-13):

> Have you forgotten that my life depends on yours? Do you reject me as a partner in the task you have undertaken? Is it because of our nuptial vows or our conjugal joy that you think that I, your wedded wife, would fail the test of climbing the frozen mountains at your side?

Put your faith in woman's strength. There is nothing that wedded love can't accomplish.

Silius' educated Roman readers would have recalled the poignant farewell between Hector, Andromache and Astyanax that takes place in Homer's *Iliad* 6. The scene also gives Hannibal the opportunity to instruct Imilce to have their son, who at the time was not yet a year old, 'place his childish hands on the altar of Elissa (i.e. Dido) and swear on his father's ashes to fight against Rome', thereby ensuring that the curse will continue from generation to generation (*Punica* 3.82f.).

Hannibal achieved modest success on the French stage. Thomas Corneille, brother of the much more famous and much more gifted Pierre, wrote an undistinguished tragedy entitled *La mort d'Annibal* (1669). Pierre de Marivaux also wrote a tragedy in five acts entitled *Annibal* (or *La mort d'Hannibal*), which takes place in the court of King Prusias of Bithynia in the final days of Hannibal's life. He also introduced a love-interest in the person of Laodice, Prusias' daughter. The play ends just as Hannibal takes poison. 'Oh how I pity you! All I lose in dying is dying itself,' Hannibal declares to Prusias, his betrayer, as he gasps his last. It was pure melodrama. First performed at the Théâtre Français on 16 December 1720, *Annibal* was such a complete flop that Marivaux never tried his hand at tragedy again.

Hannibal made a cameo appearance at the dawn of cinematic history in Giovanni Pastrone's *Cabiria* (1914), named after a Roman girl who was enslaved by the Carthaginians and narrowly escaped being sacrificed to their evil god Moloch. *Cabiria* was released soon after Italy's defeat of the Ottoman Turks in the Italo-Turkish War, which led to its acquisition of Cyrenaica and Tripolitania. Pastrone depicts Carthaginian society as barbaric and monstrous, in contrast to the nobility and enlightenment of the Romans – ample justification, the film implies, for Italy's imperialist ambitions in North Africa. Hannibal later had a subsidiary role in Carmine Gallone's

Fig. 17. Hannibal (Howard Keel) and Amytis (Esther Williams) sizing each other up in *Jupiter's Darling*, directed by George Sidney (MGM 1955).

Scipio l'africano (1937). Starring Annibale (*sic!*) Ninchi as Scipio and Camillo Pilotto as Hannibal, the production was sponsored by Benito Mussolini, who saw Scipio's invasion of Africa as precedent for his war against Abyssinia. Though the film is primarily celebrated for being an outstanding example of fascist cinema, to

Gallone's credit its propagandistic message is not overly obtrusive or offensive and there is a commendable absence of racial stereotyping. Hannibal himself is portrayed as capable of cruelty but not lacking in sensitivity. On learning of the death of his brother Mago, he delivers the following lines, which, I suspect, hit the historical mark spot on:

> A man's country is the land for which he takes chances, battles for, and he loves it. If a man's country is where he has placed all of his ambitions, why then the land itself is a reason for living. And if it's the land that can make you suffer and to abandon it is to die, then my beloved country is Italy.

Drawing on a cast of nearly 3,000 extras, 1,000 horses and 50 elephants, *Scipio l'africano* was by far the most expensive Italian film of its period. The Battle of Zama remains to this day one of the finest depictions of combat ever rendered on screen. This status was achieved in part by the butchering of many of the elephants as they stampeded into the lines of terrified extras, some of the killing being captured in vivid close-up.

George Sidney's *Jupiter's Darling* (1955) represents Hollywood's first and brashest attempt to film Hannibal's assault on Rome. This preposterous, tongue-in-cheek spoof musical, which stars Howard Keel in the leading role, is set in 216 BC. As Fabius Maximus (George Sanders) dithers and delays, as is his wont, his fiancée Amytis (Esther Williams) decides to pay an unannounced visit to Hannibal to beg for Rome's reprieve. Love blossoms and Amytis forces Hannibal to choose between capturing 'either Rome or her heart', and in so doing provides a further explanation as to why he failed to march on Rome. The film contains the following memorably unmetrical refrain, which Hannibal delivers slouched on the back of an elephant:

Fig. 18. Hannibal (Victor Mature) carrying Sylvia (Rita Gam) in
Hannibal, directed by Edgar G. Ulmar (Warner Bros 1959).

The conqueror of the world!
I've come all the way from Carthage
And I'm a long, long way from home.
But I won't go back to Carthage
Till I've battered in the gates of Rome!

Jupiter's Darling was followed in 1959 by Edgar G. Ulmar's
leaden-footed *Hannibal*, whose cast of thousands included 4,000
infantry, 1,500 cavalry and 45 elephants for the Battle of Cannae
alone. Once again the ladies get the better of our man. In this case,
however, Hannibal (Victor Mature), debonair with black eye patch,
falls for a captive Roman girl called Sylvia (Rita Gam), who just so
happens to be the fiancée of Fabius' son Quintilius. Hannibal, it
turns out, is a true Carthaginian gent. When Sylvia is brought to his

151

tent and asks him what he's going to do with her, he gallantly replies, 'First I'm going to drink a toast to your beauty.' He then takes her on a tour of his army as he might any foreign dignitary. Quintilius is far less civilised. 'Where were you last night?' he petulantly demands when she returns to Rome the next day unmolested by her captor. Spiritually enriched by her exposure to Carthaginian courtliness, Sylvia henceforth devotes herself to becoming an ambassador for global peace. 'That girl will be the ruin of us,' Hannibal's lieutenant Maharbal prophesies. And so it proves. The situation is complicated by the unexpected arrival at the camp of Hannibal's wife. Anticipating her beloved's destined demise several years later – is the audience expected to catch the allusion? – the hapless Sylvia opts to takes poison. The real stars are the elephants.

Reputedly Vin Diesel is eager both to direct and to play the leading role in a film provisionally entitled *Hannibal the Conqueror* (*sic*), which was originally due to be released in 2011. Meanwhile 20th Century Fox has been considering making an epic with Denzel Washington as Hannibal. Given the current economic climate and the failure of other epic movie ventures of late, it seems less than likely that either will see the light of day, though they have prompted animated chatter on the internet as to which (if either) star has the more appropriate skin colour for the part.

In Andrew Lloyd Webber's musical *Phantom of the Opera* (1986), *Hannibal* is the name of an invented opera by an invented composer called Chalumeau. The musical purports to include an extract from a choral scene in which Hannibal and his army return to Carthage in order to save the city from Scipio. The Carthaginian also features in several historical novels. Ross Leckie's *Hannibal: The Novel* (Washington, DC, 2006), the first of a trilogy that includes *Scipio Africanus: The Man who defeated Hannibal* (1998) and *Carthage* (2001), is a first-person account, written at the moment of Hannibal's death. Leckie emphasises the fact that Hannibal is a product of Hellenic culture, but also makes him capable of the worst brutality. A more human side to his personality is revealed by his relationship with this wife, Similce, whose rape is gruesomely and somewhat gratuitously described. Other novels include D.A. Durham's *Pride of Carthage: A Novel of Hannibal*, and Brian Todd's *Hannibal's Last Battle: Zama and the Fall of Carthage*. In 2006 the BBC produced a film called *Hannibal* starring Alexander Siddig in the title role. Documentaries include the History Channel's *The True Story of Hannibal* (2006).

In the twentieth century the Italians saw Rome's ultimate victory over the Carthaginians as an analogy for their own ultimate victory over their enemies. At the presumed site of the Battle of Lake Trasimene an inscribed brick monument erected on 24 June 1920 makes reference to Hannibal's 'inextinguishable hatred (*l'inestinguibile odio*)'. The authorities wished to draw a comparison between Trasimene and the First World War Battle of Caporetto (1917). It was at Caporetto on the northeast border of Italy that their army was heavily defeated in a surprise invasion by the combined Austro-Hungarian and German forces. Though victorious, the inscription notes, Hannibal was later vanquished at Zama. The final outcome of the Second Punic War is darkly described as 'a warning to future generations (*monito dei lontani nepoti*)', the obvious message being that the Italian army always wins in the end. Likewise the Battle of Cannae is commemorated on the banks of the River Ofante, where a modern column bears an inscription that quotes that most Churchillian of Livian sentences (22.54.10): 'Surely no other nation could have suffered such tremendous disasters and not have been destroyed.' Relations between Carthage and Rome were finally established on a secure footing (we may hope for all time) when the mayors of the two cities signed a formal pact of friendship in January 1985. The power of Hannibal's life both to inspire and warn endures.

12

The Verdict

Despite the havoc he caused, no ancient author of whom we have record vilified Hannibal. Polybius, who so admired the Romans, was in awe both of the magnitude of his achievement – he claims that the Romans outnumbered Hannibal by 40 to 1 – and of the fact that he came 'so close to success' (2.24.1). Later he writes, 'A single man, a single personality was responsible for everything that happened to both the Romans and the Carthaginians – I mean of course Hannibal' (9.22.1). In modern times Lord Montgomery of Alamein (*A History of Warfare* [London 1968] 97) asserted that '[Hannibal's] tactical genius at Cannae stands comparison with the conduct of any battle in the history of warfare', though he (rightly) deemed his overall strategy as 'a complete failure'.

Undeniably the most fascinating verdict on Hannibal would have been that of Hannibal himself, delivered first in 203 when the Carthaginian Senate ordered him out of Italy, next in 195 when he fled into exile, and last in *c.* 193 when the assassins finally caught up with him. Did it ever occur to him to reflect that his superhuman efforts had been ruinous to the state for which he had made so many sacrifices, and if so how did he confront that sobering truth? Or was he in what pop psychiatrists today would call 'a state of denial' to the end?

There are so many unanswerable questions. Was Hannibal Carthage's greatest patriot or an independent political agent with no allegiance to any cause other than his own? Though he failed in his objective, in making that crassly obvious point we have to concede that historians today continue to debate what his objective actually *was*.

Polybius says he should have first subdued the rest of the Mediterranean before turning his attention to Rome (11.19.6-7), but once he had set out from Spain in whatever direction, he would have provoked Rome in the end anyway. In other words, the outcome would have been the same, no matter how Hannibal had played his hand. Arguably the most critical error was his failure to keep up the pressure in the months after Cannae, irrespective of whether he should have marched on Rome at that point. Instead he allowed his army to dissipate its energies by collecting booty. Perhaps this was their promised payback for the rigours of the punishing march, but if so it was a colossal misjudgement on his part.

He made several other misjudgements. He miscalculated the degree of support that he would receive from the Gauls, in part as a result of having failed to generate much enthusiasm within their ranks, despite their initial eagerness for his cause. He was convinced that Rome's confederation would crumble following the military defeats. He placed too much trust in the expectation that his brother Hasdrubal would bring reinforcements from Spain in timely fashion. He stayed on in southern Italy long after there was any hope that he could reverse the course of events.

But there were failings as well as misjudgements. One was his lacklustre performance as a besieger, which was only partly due to his lack of siege equipment. As Peddie (*Hannibal's War* [Stroud 1997] 196) notes, in the crucial years from 218 to 215 he besieged thirteen towns but succeeded in taking only four. Had his engineers possessed the techniques to storm the many towns he invested, and had he been able to convince his army of the crucial value of such an undertaking, he might just have succeeded. But he also lacked adequate manpower to undertake a protracted siege. Military historians estimate that it requires an army that is three times larger than the number of defenders to besiege a town successfully, and Hannibal was never able to tie up a force of that size for very long. A further handicap was his indebtedness to his Italian allies, which prevented him from remaining in one place for long and thus distracted him from his primary goal. As a result, having captured a town, he was often unable to keep hold of it. It took him months to starve out the small town of Casilinum but he held it for under two years. He seems not to have given any logistical support to either Hasdrubal or Mago when they arrived in Italy with reinforcements. He had no fallback plan in the event that his mission failed. He did not grasp the potential benefit of taking the war into Sicily.

He largely lost the propaganda war in Italy. After each of his three major victories he released his non-Roman prisoners, claiming that he was fighting against the Romans for the freedom of Italy (Polybius 3.77.4-7; 3.85.4; Livy 22.58.1-2). Lazenby has argued that at some point or another in the course of his campaign 40% of Rome's allies defected. Yet this proved insufficient to alter the course of the conflict. Though a number of Rome's allies in the south of Italy joined his cause after Cannae, those who lived in the centre and the north remained loyal, largely due to the fact that they saw little to gain by switching sides. Another reason why Hannibal was unable to detach a larger proportion was because he failed to appreciate the difference in political status between the non-Latins and the Latin colonies. The non-Latins were bound to Rome by a hotchpotch of treaties and alliances, and this made it virtually impossible for them to unite in a common cause. The Latins derived considerable benefit from their attachment to Rome. Not a single Latin colony went over to Hannibal's side.

Manifestly, Hannibal's victories failed to decide the outcome of the war. The strategy he applied after Cannae resulted in a stalemate, and only once thereafter did he pose a genuine threat to Rome. Had he acknowledged that fact, cut his losses, and returned to Africa with his army largely intact even as late as 205, Carthage might not have lost the war, though the thirteen years after Cannae should by no means be judged a complete failure. If, too, his brother Hasdrubal had succeeded in joining forces with him in 207, the war might have gone his way. Hannibal, however, was manifestly a one-man show. No Carthaginian general came remotely close to him in either tactical ability or sheer doggedness.

The end of the Hannibalic War was not, of course, the end of the road for Hannibal, and it is immensely to his credit that he later directed his energy towards the good of the Carthaginian people by reforming its ailing economy and paying off the crippling war debt. He also sought to eradicate the abuses of the wealthy, who were off-loading the majority of that debt upon those least able to bear the burden. It might in fact with justification be claimed that he was much more successful as a politician than he had been as a general.

Ancient historians today rightly refrain from passing a moral verdict on the ancients. Gilbert Abbott à Beckett, author of *The Comic History of Rome* (1852), images from whose work appear in this book (Figs 3, 5 and 6), described him as 'a miserable specimen of ill-regulated humanity', on the grounds that he was 'more skilful in the art of exterminating his fellow-creatures than many of his competitors' (p. 202). As we noted in the first chapter, however, there are surprisingly few reports of brutality, and none that suggest he engaged in genocide.

Hannibal encountered the ancient world in all its diversity and was, so far as we can tell, largely unburdened by prejudice, at least by the admittedly low standards of his age. He was acquainted with a mixture of cultures – Iberian, Celtic, Italian, Latin, Numidian, Libyan, Greek and Armenian, as well as Punic. He was what we would call today a global citizen – a man whose mindset represented a complex synthesis of many of the cultures that flourished in the

Mediterranean world of his day. If anyone from antiquity could have communicated what it meant to cross cultural boundaries, that man was Hannibal.

Outstanding though he was in pitched battle, original and creative though he was in unconventional operational theatres, and adept though he was in interpreting the mindset of his adversaries, Hannibal never delivered the fatal body blow. Despite the heroic grandeur of his march across the Alps, and the series of spectacular victories that he secured in under two years, the rest was indeed failure, albeit failure on a magnificent scale.

Finally, Hannibal was indisputably one of the greatest survivors that the ancient world produced. The march across the Alps in atrocious conditions accompanied by elephants and a motley, polyglot army, lacking a compass or a map and repeatedly under attack from hostile tribes, was one of the most heroic ever undertaken. He set a standard for what is humanly possible that has hardly been exceeded, and he remains an inspiration to this day in terms of his physical and psychological endurance. He was Rome's greatest adversary in every sense of the term. The ultimate tragedy, both for himself and, arguably too, for Carthage, is that he did not die at the peak of his powers.

Further Reading

Of the books devoted exclusively to Hannibal I recommend Sir Gavin De Beer's *Hannibal: The Struggle for Power in the Mediterranean* (London 1969) as the best place to start. De Beer breezes along amiably. He is very strong on the geography and there is a lot of useful, if somewhat basic, background information on Carthage. Almost every page has an illustration – this, after all, is a Thames and Hudson book. His maps are not much use but there are some interesting photos of the terrain Hannibal passed through. Serge Lancel's *Hannibal* (Oxford 1998) offers a straightforward biography, very detailed, but occasionally discursive and meandering. Though the blurb suggests that he is writing from the perspective of Carthage, that challenge is hardly attainable. Nevertheless, Lancel does his best to re-create Hannibal's world and mental world-view. Dexter Hoyos' *Hannibal: Rome's Greatest Enemy* (Exeter 2008) is highly readable and shows deep insight into its subject's character. K. Christ's *Hannibal* (Darmstadt 1974), in German, is a very useful collection of essays.

Theodore Ayrault Dodge's two-volume work *Hannibal: A History of the Art of War among the Carthaginians and Romans down to the Battle of Pydna in 168 BC, with a Detailed Account of the Second Punic War*, first published in 1891, is still in print. Dodge served on the Union side at the Battle of Gettysburg and though his book is something of a period piece it is still highly impressive. As he notes in the Preface he made many visits to 'the scenes of the Punic captain's achievements' and his detailed hand-drawn illustrations alone make this work an incomparable resource. Dexter Hoyos' *Hannibal's Dynasty: Power and Politics in the Western Mediterranean 247-183 BC* (London and New York 2003) gives plentiful attention to the entire Barcid clan, including Hamilcar, Hasdrubal and Hannibal. Noting the interesting fact that all three men exercised dominance not in their homeland but abroad in either Spain or Italy, the author explores the means by which the structures of Carthaginian politics and Carthage's relations with neighbouring peoples made their achievements possible. He is also good in exposing the bias of the ancient sources. Leonard Cottrell's *Hannibal: Enemy of Rome* (New York 1960) is still a good read. Cottrell, who has a no-nonsense style of writing, declares that he 'fulfilled a lifetime's ambition' before writing his book, namely by tracing Hannibal's footsteps from Cartagena to Rome by car.

Top of my list of the scholarly books on the Punic Wars is Adrian Goldsworthy's *The Punic Wars* (London 2000). His descriptions of the battles are first-rate and his maps are excellent, and he writes in an engaging and lively style. J.F. Lazenby's *Hannibal's War* (Warminster, 1978; pbk 1998) is also excellent, notwithstanding the fact that he modestly alludes to his 'impertinence' in writing about 'one of the great commanders of history' without having experienced battle first-hand himself (equally true of me, though I did learn how to clean a rifle and strip a Bren gun at school). The Preface to the paperback edition contains a valuable annotated bibliography on the most relevant articles to date. Dexter Hoyos' *Unplanned Wars: the Origins of the First and Second Punic Wars* (Berlin and New York 1998) scrupulously assesses Hannibal's responsibility for the outbreak of the Second Punic War. Brian Caven's *The Punic Wars* (London and New York 1980) is admirably detailed, despite the absence of references or notes. John Peddie's *Hannibal's War* (Stroud 1997) is informative on a variety of logistical details, including Hannibal's fighting strength, allied contributions, number of elephants, etc. Its many glossy illustrations include paintings, etchings and drawings of Hannibal. He ends with the Battle of Zama. Dennis Proctor's *Hannibal's March in History* (Oxford 1971) is essential reading for anyone fascinated by both chronological and geographical questions, even though many of his conclusions remain speculative. In *Hannibal Crosses the Alps: The Invasion of Italy and the Second Punic War* (Cambridge, MA 1998) John Prevas, an experienced rock climber, discusses the merits of all the passes that Hannibal might have taken through the Alps and ultimately casts his vote for the highest and most inaccessible of them all, namely the Col de la Traversette. Adrian Goldsworthy's *Cannae* (London 2001) provides a background to Hannibal's greatest battle and is amply illustrated. G. Daly's *Cannae: The Experience of Battle in the Second Punic War* (London 2002) analyses the two different military systems and the technicalities of warfare. V. Hanson's essay on 'Cannae' in R. Cowley's *The Experience of War* (London 1992) makes an imaginative attempt to depict the final stages of the battle.

H.H. Scullard's chapter 'The Carthaginians in Spain' (pp. 17-43) and John Briscoe's 'The Second Punic War' (pp. 44-80) in the *Cambridge Ancient History* (2nd edn, vol. VIII: *Rome and the Mediterranean to 133 BC* [Cambridge 1989]) are authoritative, although overall Hannibal receives short shrift in the *CAH*. G. de Sanctis' *Storia dei Romani* (2nd edn, vol. III part 2 [Florence 1968]) is still the most magisterial account of the war. I also recommend T. Cornell, B. Rankov and B. Sabin's *The Second Punic War: A Reappraisal* (= *Bulletin of the Institute of Classical Studies* supplement no. 67 [London 1996]), a collection of papers on some of the most contested issues concerning the war. Particularly germane to the present work are John Lazenby's 'Was Maharbal right?' (pp. 39-47) and Tim Cornell's 'Hannibal's legacy: the effects of the Hannibal war in Italy' (pp. 97-113). H.H. Scullard's *Scipio Africanus: Soldier and Politician* (London 1970) is important for the campaign in Spain and Africa.

Elephant enthusiasts can hardly do better than consult his *The Elephant in the Greek and Roman World* (London 1974).

Mention should also be made of Gustave Flaubert's historical novel *Salammbô, roman carthaginois* (1862), which is set in Carthage at the time of the so-called Mercenaries' War (237-233 BC). It is named after a (suppositious) daughter of Hamilcar. Flaubert devoted five years researching the topic and made four trips to Carthage, the first in 1857. He was powerfully affected by the exotic atmosphere of north Africa, and though the 'hero' of the novel is Hamilcar Barca, there's no evidence that Flaubert had any particular interest in his son Hannibal.

The best introduction to Carthage is Serge Lancel's *Carthage: A History* (Oxford 1995), which provides a history of the city from its foundation to its destruction, as well as an account of its survival through archaeology and fiction. Lancel spent many years excavating in and around Carthage, so his discussion of the archaeological data is especially illuminating. Particularly valuable are ch. 6 'Religion' and ch. 8 'Between East and West: an ambiguous cultural identity', the latter being an exploration of the complex roots of Carthaginian cultural identity. Lancel (p. 442) notes that Flaubert's *Salammbô* did much to promote the cause of Carthaginian archaeology. Gilbert and Colette Charles-Picard, *Daily Life in Carthage in the Time of Hannibal* (tr. A.E. Foster [London 1961]) is, despite its age, still satisfactory. Though only one of its chapters actually lives up to the title, it provides an informative and well-balanced discussion of Carthage's social structure, economy, culture and religion. B.H. Warmington's *Carthage* (Harmondsworth 1969) offers a useful introduction, though what is potentially its most instructive chapter, 'The city of Carthage and its political and religious life' (ch. 6), is dated. *Carthage: L'histoire, sa trace, et son écho* (no author given, Paris 1995) contains two chapters that are highly relevant for our understanding of the culture that produced Hannibal, namely 'Splendeurs de Carthage' and 'Des guerres puniques à la chute de Carthage' (chs 2 and 3 respectively, both by various authors). These are extremely well-illustrated and provide an excellent picture of the opulence and sophistication of Carthaginian society. José de los Llanos' essay entitled 'L'image des héros des guerres puniques à l'époque moderne' (*op. cit.*, pp. 170-80) explores Hannibal's afterlife in art and literature. For the Phoenicians, see M.E. Aubet, *The Phoenicians and the West: Politics, Colonies and Trade* (Cambridge 1993; 2nd edn 2001). The entry under 'Phoenicians' in *Brill's New Pauly* (vol. XI cols 148-69 [Leiden and Boston 2007]) is useful.

For Hannibal's legacy (political, social, economic, and ecological), Arnold Toynbee's two-volume work, *Hannibal's Legacy: The Hannibalic War's Effects on Roman Life* (London 1965), is unrivalled, even though its investigative parameters extend way beyond what many scholars would comfortably acknowledge to be an identifiable relationship between cause and effect. But while its more extravagant claims have been challenged by Peter Brunt's highly influential *Italian Manpower, 225 BC-AD 14* (Oxford 1971; 2nd edn 1987), it still has a great deal to offer.

The major sources in translation include *Hannibal's War: Books XXI-XXXI of Livy* (translated by J.C. Yardley with introduction and notes by D. Hoyos [Oxford 2006]), and *Polybius: The Rise of the Roman Empire* (tr. I. Scott-Kilvert, selected with intro. by F.W. Walbank [Penguin 1979]). F.W. Walbank's *A Historical Commentary on Polybius* in 3 vols. (Oxford 1957, 1967 and 1979) is an extremely useful and highly detailed accompaniment, even for those without knowledge of Greek. *Livy: The War with Hannibal* (tr. A. De Sélincourt, edited with introduction by B. Radice [Penguin 1972]) is also valuable but lacks notes. For Appian, I recommend J.S. Richardson, *Appian: Wars of the Romans in Iberia* (Warminster 2000), a parallel Greek and Latin text, whose commentary is informative for Hannibal's early years in Spain. For those with some knowledge of Latin there is Brian Beyer's *War with Hannibal: Authentic Latin Prose for the Beginning Student* (New Haven and London 2009). This is a basic edition of Book 3 of Eutropius' *Breviarium ab urbe condita,* which covers the Second Punic War.

Finally, for anyone who like myself has a boundless passion for Hannibal, I recommend Bernard Levin's *Hannibal's Footsteps* (London 1985), which was produced in conjunction with a Channel 4 television series of the same name. With great reluctance, the author tells us, he abandoned the idea of re-tracing Hannibal's epic journey on the back of an elephant.

As Dr Johnson observed of a much-loved friend, if I had a dog I should name him Hannibal.

Index

Index

Made in the USA
Middletown, DE
05 June 2021

41179014R00095